Fred Crocker

The only complete directory of the poultry, pigeon & pet stock breeders in the United States of America

Fred Crocker

The only complete directory of the poultry, pigeon & pet stock breeders in the United States of America

ISBN/EAN: 9783337147150

Printed in Europe, USA, Canada, Australia, Japan

Cover: Foto ©Lupo / pixelio.de

More available books at **www.hansebooks.com**

THE . ONLY COMPLETE

DIRECTORY

—— OF THE ——

Poultry, Pigeon & Pet Stock

BREEDERS

—— IN THE ——

UNITED STATES OF AMERICA

PRESS OF FRED. HALLETT,
YARMOUTHPORT, MASS.

DIRECTORY.

ALABAMA.

Boggess B M, Indranola, pit games
Brister W D, Pleasant Hill, lang, leg
Freeman E P, Alpine, game
Gregory P E & Co, 2009 First Ave, Birmingham
McCrafferty Mrs, H J, Birmingham, wy
Rugsdale W B, Florence, f f
Time Isaac W, Mayapple f f

ARKANSAS.

Cross M C, Pine Bluff
Cross & Russell, Pine Bluff
Deeners R S, Batesville, bra, p r, etc

BRITISH COLUMBIA.

Kirk C W, Victoria, f f
Livingstone W, Savonas Ferry, f f
Leech W H, Sherman, f f
Parks Nelson, Parksville, f f

CONNECTICUT.

Alsop J W, Middleton, i g
Andrews F H, Woodstock, f f
Allen M M, Porter Ashe, g
Bailey R G, Rockville, f f
Burr R H, Middletown, p cochins
Boardman F E, Little River, wy, p r
Bishop J D, Torrington, b p r
Brandt H B, Manchester, f f
Babcock F W, Tyler City, f f
Blinn D F, Buckland, f f
Benton A G, Guilford f f
Beach E E, E Hartford, f f
Buddington E F, Rockville f f
Bunnell C W, South Beach f f
Bruce J E, Windsor, f f
Burmingham H D,
Bartlet C P, Brookwater, f f
Barnes C W, Stafford, s b polish
Baldwin J E, South Bevey, langshans
Carpenter A E, Putnam, l brahmas
Crosby C H, Bridgeport, f f
Clark & Barnes, Plymouth f f
Comins C W, Stafford Springs, b s polish
Cowles A F, Manchester, f f
Crosby F T, Middletown, l brahmas
Clark E, Hysanum, Langshans
Chamberlin Rev, Walter, East Village, f f

Dodge W D, Ansonia, f f
Day A L, Saybrook, g
Driscoll C T, New Haven, f f
Dean G W, New Haven f f
Davis H W, Wellingford, s l wy
Dorn White, E, Haddam, f f
Faucher A A, Danbury, i g
Farnham, A N, New Haven, f f
Francis G A, Bridgeport, f f
Fairchild H L, Nichols, f f
Forbes, N D, New Haven, f f
Fancier N E, Danielsonville, lang
Grant Frank H, Rockville, w p r
Gaul J, Warehouse Point f f
Hart A M, Meriden, w p r
Horton P A, Cheshire
Hartwell Sherman, Washington, f f
Howard C A, Wilsonville, wy, leg
Hendrick H D, Birmingham, Bantams
Hilditch Wm Jr, Thompsonville, leg
Hale J Willar, E Hartford, w p r
Hamilton W H, Danielsonville, lang
Harris W H, Southington, f f
Hawkins Sam, Whigville, f f
Houghtaling, Sharon Falls, p r, wy g
Hurlburt & Norton, Kensington, f f
Jenney B T, Manchester Green, b l, etc
Jordan C P
Kingsley John, Meriden, lang
King John W, Kent, leg, w p r
Kupt & Son, Middletown, f f
Kleit Wm & Son, Middleton
Leach Geo W, Rockville, f f
Lacy E A, Bridgeport, brown leg
Luckwood Fred, Stanwich, f f
Long Daniel C, Coventry, f f
Mitchell Geo W, Bristol, p c
Mitchell & Russell, Bristol, w c
Manson J E, Fair Haven, f f
Messenger C E, Winsted, wy
McLean C L, Rockville, lang
Manson L E, New Haven f f
Noble W N, Collinsville, f f
Nettleton John F, New Haven, f f
Nichols D A, Monroe, f f
Neal W H, Southington, f f
O'Connell F M, New Haven, f f
Phelps I H, Whethersfield, w & b p r

Pease W A, Middleton, f f
Parker John, New Haven, f f
Pratt Geo S, Bridgeport, f f
Robinson W H, East Haven f f
Stoddard J G, Nervington Junction, f f
Seeley & Nicholas, Bridgeport, f f
Stoddard H H, Hartford, f f
Shute W H, Middletown, w wy
Sherwood Frank, Hartford, b p r
Spaulding M J, E Hartford, l b
Shute J & Son, Meriden, wy
Sturtevant F C
Smith Bros, Deep River, f f
Sharp J E & A R, Taunton, f f
Spaulding M J, Brookwater, f f
Shephard A L, Brookfield, f f
Todd F A, New Haven, f f
Todd A B, Centerville, f f
Tatt G E, Unionville, f f
Wright Jewett, Suffield, g
Webster A B, Bristol w p r
Williams A F, Bristol, f f
Webb C C, Bristol, p r & p d
Wirsley Geo M, Windsor, f f
Watson Reed, East Windsor Hill, leg
Woodruff W W, Watertown, f f
Webber John G Jr, Berlin f f
Wells Wm A, Norwich, f f

CALIFORNIA.

Anderson M L, Trepico, Los Angeles, Langshans
Apel Mrs John Alameda, bra, etc
Albie O J, Lawrence, lang, p r etc
Bingham F T, Los Angeles, f f
Brown James F, Los Angeles, f f
Bordwell H W, East Riverside, f f
Babcock H S, f f
Badger Geo B, Santa Cruz, f f
Bowers Mrs J H, Boka, f f
Crawford All, San Bernardino, lang
Critcher Madison H, Bonnie Doon, bea, etc
Clapp E C, Pasadena, f f
Conger Sid, f f
Crosby C H, f f
Collins Chas W, Boyle Heights, f f
Condee Robt A, San Bernardino, f f
Dellwood Poultry Yards, Napa, wy bra, pr etc
Davis B F & G C, Orange, f f
Dorland R I, French Cam, f f
Dodge C B, Blue Lake, lang
Dwight W H, Pasadena, f f
Ellis Ed, Santa Rosa, bra, p r, etc
Eringer F A, Sheridan, f f
Edmonson Jas, San Bernardino, f f
Farrester Henry, Las Amine, lang
Fink A W, San Francisco, p ducks
Freeman E H, Santa Clara, pr etc
Fithian Miss Frances C, Glendale, f f
Green Anthony, Sacramento, f f
Haight Marshall, Anaheim, red caps, etc
Hagan John, Hurneme, f f
Harker Chas R, Santa Clara, w p r
Haddox J T, El Monte, f f
Hunt Ralph, Pasadena, f f
Hehan John, Hueneme, f f
Hageman Gus, Dow's Prairie, f f
Johnston C F, Santa Anna, f f
Jones W H H, Pasadena, f f
Jones Mrs James A, Oakland, leg, H
Jones M L, Sacramento, f f

Keesling H G, San Jose, f f
Lewelling H J, St Helena, r caps
McFadden Mrs Flora, Santa Anna, f f
McFarling John, Oakland, Bra, p r etc
Mitchell James, St Helena, wy
Mercer John, Los Angeles, f f
McGunn F F Jr, f f
Moore Albert, Santa Anna, f f
Minassian Hicks, Santa Barbara, f f
Niles Wm, Maple Ave & Washington St, Los Angeles, f f
Nisson C, Petaluma, leg
Nash J D, Pasadena, f f
Oakland Poultry Yards, Oakland, f f
O'Neill R V, Pasadena, f f
Peer Geo E, f f
Paul C F, 122 W First St, Los Angeles, f f
Perry C A, Santa Rosa, f f
Richardson Wm H, San Francisco, f g
Ruschhaupt A C, Los Angeles, f f
Rutledge James, Santa Anna, f f
Rowan Robert, Pasadena, f f
Scotten Orren, f f
Spaulding E R, f f
Shears C H, Sacremento, g f
Sebastopol L G C, f f
Shaw B H, Station R, Los Angeles, f f
Sylvester Mrs, Santa Anna, f f
Strong N E, Pensona, f f
Thomas W H, National City, f f
Toyne G, Castro Valley, f f
Thomas J H L, Los Angeles, f f
Tyler S, Oak Glen, Pasadena, wy d
Thurston W W, Los Angeles, f f
Terwellinger E R, r g
Thurber E Carlton, Alhambra, i g
Urmy Dr H N, Los Angeles, f f
Whitney W W, Glendale, f f
Wear Mrs F, Bakersfield, f f
White & Wood, Danville, f f
Young W W, Villa Park, f f

CANADA.

Allin Bros, Newcastle, Ont, b & w p r
Arthens Wm, Toronto, lang
Bartlett & George, London Ont, leg
Barber W & Co 242 Queen St, W Toronto, b b r g
Bornseville W Danville, P Q, b b r g f
Bartlett Thomas, Angus, Ont, lang
Bauldwin Claude, E Barnston, Que, s wy etc
Bong W G, London, Ont, wyan
Bogue G Strathroy, b c
Bonnick Chas, Toronto, g bantams
Bennett J E, Toronto, b p r
Cockburn T Jr, Canada St, Hamilton, f f
Clemo S M Dunnville, Ont, p r, wy
Charlesworth, H M, Owen Sound, p r
Carnew W, Belleville, p g
Cuthberston Robt, W Belhaven, Ont, y m br, turkeys
Comrt & Spittigne, Tecumseth House, London, g & s wy
Concordan J L, Stratford, Ontario, b p r
Coon Wm, Guelph, Ont, b m, wh leg
Clerno S M Dunnville, Ont, w p r, wy, etc
Cameron Bros, Horner, Ont, b r g bantams
Clark J B, Dunnville, Ont, f f
Donovan H R, Toronto, Ont, lang
Daniels J C, Toronto, Cornish i g
Davies G D, Toronto, Ont, i g
Duff Thomas A, Toronto, Ont, b & w m

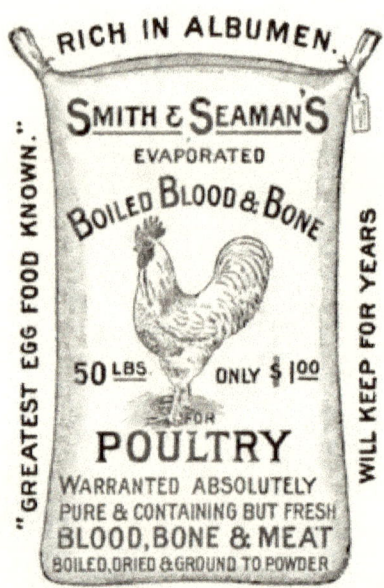

Doty E F, Toronto, g b, etc
Duncan John, Collingwood, b lang
Dunn Geo, Woodstock, Ont, canaries
Duke Henry R, Toronto, f f
Evans R W, London, Ont, c, leg, wyan
Edsall L W Selkirk, l & d br
Eckardt C W, Ridgeville, Ont, p r
Elliott & Mc Leod, London, Ont, b & w pr
Erzebe C J, Guelph, Ont, lang
Fleming C D, Chatham, Ont, b c
Fendly Wm, Brampton, Ont, b l
Flint F, Toronto, Ont, p d
Fox W, Toronto, pigeons
Geddes Alfred, Ottawa, f f
Graham A W, St Thomas, Ont, s c w leg
Goode G T, Fort Erie, Ont, leg
Gracey R J, Wellandport, Ont, wyan
Gray John, Tornorden, Ont, w w, p r
Hamler Geo H, Tilsonburg, Ont, l f
Hare F C, Whitby Ont, b c
Hall C H & Co, King City, Ont, f f
Hope Geo & Sons, Toronto, singing birds
Hall Wm, Napanee, Ont, w p r
Haycock & Rent, Cataraqui, Ont, g & w w
Hart Philip, Belleville, Ont, m, etc
Hern J M, Bowmanville, l b, p c, etc
Hall Ed, Markhams, leg
Jackson C S, Ontario, b & p c & l b
Jackman S & P, Bowmanville, Ont, b c
Kelley T J, London, Ont, p c
Keyes P G, Ottawa, Ont, s wy, b c
Laing Geo, Milton, West, Ont, f f
Loneks Mrs N A, Dresden, canaries
Longhrey Wm A, London, l l
Lander Mrs N S, Ottawa, Ont, f f
Murphy E F, Ottawa, b r ban
Mc Gaw W H, Hamilton, bra
Millard R B, London, Ont
Mc Cartney W F, Bethany, Ont, leg etc
Meyer J E, Kossuth, Ont, Wyan
Marshall R H, Dunnville, p c
Martin & Mander, Unionville, Ont, l b
Mc Cormick Geo G, London, b c, etc
Mc Kinlay A R, Deer Park, Ont, f f
Noble John A, Nowal, Ont, i g, w & g l w
O'Brien & Colwell, Paris Station, Ont, l & d b
Odell W S, Ottawa, S S H am, p d
Otter E J, 90 Degrassi St, Toronto, d b, leg, etc
O'Neil J J, Coaticook Qu, w w, lang, etc
Pequegnat Leon G, New Hamburg, Ont, b p r
Patterson Walter Jr, Barrie, Ont, p ban
Pierce Henry R, Strathroy, Ont, h
Plumridge Wm, Chatham, Ont, l b
Rice Thomas, Whitby, Ont, leg, m, etc
Robson C S, London, Ont, b p b
Robinson A M, London, Ont, b & W leg
Roy J R, Coaticook, Qu, b, w, etc
Robertson D, Guelph, b j
Richardson W B, Chatham, f f
Stapleford S, Watford, Ont, f f
Schlichter J, Washington, Ont, l b
Scott Wm B, Milford, Ont, f f
Thompson J A C, Gananoque, Ont, p f
Thompson J H, Whitby, l b
Trollope Robt, Singhampton, Ont, p c
Trew D C, Lindsay, Ont, Houdans
Thompson A, Prov Qu, p r
Taylor Jno A King, Ont, b c

Ulley Wm, Victoria, Square, Montreal, b p r
Vidal E A, Sarnia, Ont, b p r, etc
Wallace H H, Woodstock, Ont, w p r
Wilson Geo, Guelph, Ont, l b
Wright W & A, Richmond Hill, Ont, b c
Zavitz E M, Ravenswood, Ham, wy, etc

COLORADO.

Allen R B, Hartsel, f f
Allen E S, Loveland, f f
Allen D D, Clovanont, f f
Aldce O J, Lawrence, lang
Barber L J, Evans, f f
Brown W G, Roggen, f f
Bashor W L, Hygene, f f
Beebe J E, Denver, i g
Buckingham C G, Boulder, f f
Beecher H M, Cannon City, f f
Baker F R, Fort Collins, f f
Bloom F G, Trinidad, f f
Cockrell R M, Monte Vista, t f
Clark M R, Greely, f f
Church J, Buena Vista, f f
Clifford G A, Duel, f f
Chew E R, Pueblo, f f
Dyar O P, Laird, f f
Dudley J R, Aspen, f f
Day J L, Durango, f f
Eaton L C, Buena Vista, f f
Felker W S, Eads, f f
Ferguson Geo, Ferguson, f f
Frees J C, Montrose, f f
Fraker C F, Gypsum, t f
Green W, Hastings, f f
Guff R, Earle, f f
Grider L M, Downey, f f
Gardner J M, Del Norte, f f
Hatfield Chas, Aspen, f f
Hallett Teresa, Pagora Springs, f f
Hawkins J S, Durango, f f
Jaynes L J, Sagnache, f f
Jacobs G M, Dillon, f f
Johnston I W, Aspen, f f
Jett Chas H, Hartsell, f f
Jenkins S N R, Mosca, f f
Morris H O, Pueblo, f f
Margmardt F A, Lyons, f f
Mc Intire A W, La Java, f f
Miller J J, Durango, f f
May J K, Sterling, f f
Mc Intosh G R, Longmont, f f
Meehan M, Lyman, f f
Miller C P, La Junta, f f
Newby Alex, Salida, f f
Otis W D, Otis, f f
Oliver N H, Eaton, t f
Ostensen O E, Grand Junction, f f
Obrien H T, Colo Springs,
Parks J J, Wichata, f f
Robinson E M, Walsenburg, f f
Randall W H F, Barr, f f
Selimaog F, Buffalo Creek, f f
Snyder J J, Parachute, f f
Smith Geo, Idaho Springs, f f
Smith Geo H, Idaho Springs, i g, leg
Smith C L, Loveland, f f
Tierman Mrs Mamie, Las Amnias, f f
Thompson M, Hardin, f f
Tomlin W E, Cotton Creek, f f
Tass Frodd, Bessemer, f f
Topliam J W, Sedalia, f f

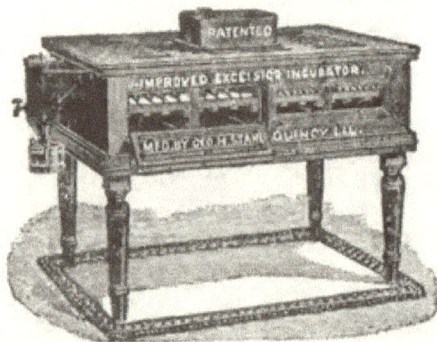

Taylor W W, Wenona, f f
White A D. Brighton, f f
Wauless J F Brighton, f f
Watson J, Aspen, f f
Warner G W, Ft Morgan, f f

DELAWARE.
Emerson P. Wyoming, s l wy
Fairley J B, Camden, f f
Fell A J. Pleasant Hill, w c b p
Hartwell E E, Wilmington, f f
Hellings J P, Dover, p r. wy, leg, ham
Hicken S M, Delaware City, w p r
McMahon Jno W, Washington, f f
Tatnal Richard R, Wilmington, i g
Thomas H M, Camden, f f
Seeney Fred H, Kenton, f f
Smith H F, Clayton, f f
McDowell L P, Middletown, p r

DAKOTA.
Doane F M, Eureka, g
Davidson Mrs Robt M, Davidson, f f
Fossum A W, Aberdeen, p r & br

ENGLAND.
Ashford Fred Saxmundham, pig
Abbott Bros, Norfolk, i g
Bonaventum Poultry Farm, Nursling, So Hampton
Consyns Alex, 273 Stuart St, London, f f
McNeilW, 114 Waterloo St, London, f f
Nixon James, Brampton Cumberland, p g
Oke Richard, Brough's Bridge, London wy, etc
Watmough J E, Bradford, Yorkshire, f f

FLORIDA.
Amsden E W. Ormond, i g wy
Foster F G, Wilaka, f f
Givens D B, Tampa, f f
Laming Dr John T, Matanzis, f f
Lynes & Co, Grove City, f f
Neff J B. Green Cove Springs, f f
Van Derver J H, Rutledge, f f

GEORGIA.
Agritola R J T, Manetta, b p r
Brown & Wadley, Bolingbroke, l & w f
Cook Ellison R, Clinton, lang
Cook Phil Jr, Lesburgh, w lang
Central Georgia Poultry Farm, Bolingbroke
Edmunds Mrs M J Elberton, p ducks, etc
Faber E S, Columbus, f f
Kurns H A, Atlanta. w p r
Lloyd W J, Social Circle, p ducks
Nichols David, Atlanta, s c b leg
Scott & Tanner, Rome, l br, etc
Williams Roger, Atlanta, w wy

INDIANA.
Aring John B, Richmond, l bra, w p r
Andrew J W, Warren, w wy, etc
Anderson A A, Boone, p r, etc
Barnard Capt, Westland, lang
Bradshaw H ... hanon, lang
Bratton R J, Dana, e, etc
Bond A S, Fort Wayne, f f
Berler C C & Son, Clifton, w p r
Burkher, Shelbyville, f f
Burke Maggie, Liberty, f f
Belden M L, La Grange, f f
Brandt A, Indianapolis, f f

Bennett J, Sunman, f f
Bradshaw H A, Elizaville, w wy, lang
Barnhart F E, Walkerton, wh leg
Benfood W P, Westland, l bra, etc
Bolinger W H, Pendleton, l bra
Barker I X, Thorntown, l bra, b p r
Boyles W N, Greensburg, l bra, b c
Burdick Frank, Tremont, lang
Bowlers Mrs J W, Williamsport, lang
Cowes S F, Thorntown, p r, wy bra, leg
Cook J W, Poncto, wy, leg
Clove W R, Trafalgar, l bra, p c
Cuningham & Co, Bunker Hill, b p r
Christian Daniel, Roanoke, p r, etc
Clarke H P, Indianapolis, i g
Cummings Alex W, Derby, f f
Crocket Ben W, Delphin, f f
Colvin John B, Curtisville, f f
Calvert, Warsaw, f f
Crockett, R W, Indianapolis, f f
Conger Sid, Flat Rock, l bra
Caldwell Jas H, Terrehaute, f f
Duncan Jno H, Linevilla, f f
Denny Samuel, Indianapolis, g wy
Dimris Harvey, Roanoke, w p r
Frving S E, Lebanon, l bra, p c
Exsley Tilman, New Market, buff c
Emrich & Dreschel, Indianapolis, b l
Erdelmeyer Frank, Indianapolis, Tumblers.
Forsyth A J, Ninevah, p r
Franci-co C L, Sayre, f f
Frints Mattie, North Judson, f f
Fleischer C W, New Albany, f f
Flickinger C J, Huntington, lang
Gilbert F M, Evansville, w fantail pigeons
Gessel E E, Muncie, wy
Griffin Major, Manzy, bra
Gordon G P, Fort Wayne, bra
Garwood E C, Richmond, leg, e
Homer J F, Monon, b p r
Highley D F, Mier, l bra
Howe J B, Kentland, p r
Hasson & Son, Indianapolis, f f
Huddleston A F, Winchester, f f
Hill B F, Indianapolis, blk c
Harconst J R, New Augusta, w wy
Hayworth Emma, Muncie, f f
Hamlin & Shafer, Pleasant Lake, lang, etc
Jones W H, Liberty, f f
Johnson C H, Rushville, buff c
Jones Jas. Swanington, f f
Johnson S A, No Vernon, f f
Kaquess H G, Poseyville, f f
Kems N A, Fairmount, p r, wy, c
Lave s A, & l N, Zorisville, l bra, wy
Lilly & Stalnaker, Indianapolis, bantams
Lane S B, Spiceland, f f
Lee J Henry, Indianapolis, f f
Lowes Nettie, Mace, f f
Lane D H, Colfax, f f
Lane S B, New Castle, f f
Lott O A & Co, Richmond, red caps
Myer Will Mrs, Bentley, lang
Myers Ben S, Crawfordsville, lang
McDougall F W, Indianapolis, p g
Melrose R, Wabash, pigeons
Masten Cyrus H, Plainfield, f f
Morris John C, Dublin, f f
Milliken H F, Danville, f f
Moore Kate, Linton, f f
McClain, W H & Son, Greenwood, p r

J. W. SHAW,
BREEDER OF LIGHT BRAHMAS,
EXCLUSIVELY,
Brockton, Mass.

CHICKS FOR SALE AFTER OCT. 1st.

LIST OF PREMIUMS WON THIS SEASON:

At Brockton: I won First and Second on Cockerels; Second on Cock; First and Second on Hens; First and Second on Pullets; First and Third on Collection; also Nine Specials.

At Boston's Great Light Brahma Show: I won First on Cockerel; Second for Best Cockerel and Four Best Pullets; Third for Best Cock and Four Best Hens; also Third on Pullet, Fourth on Hen, Fifth on Cock and Sixth and Seventh on Pullets.

Meredith A E, West Indianapolis, f f
Maisch E N, Frankfort, j g
Masten C H, Awo, f f
Myers Geo B, Richmond, c, **br, p r**
Messner C L, Williamsport, **w p r, etc**
Milhorus C R, Plainfield, leg
Melle Henry, Richmond, g f
Martin J J & Co, No Manchester, f f
Murphy E R, Carmel, leg
Nash F E, Fort Wayne, b lang
Norris Jacob, Crawfordsville, **f f**
Owsley W J, Darlington, b p r, etc
Osburn W J, Red Bridge, f f
Purdy Seth & Co, Aventon, f f
Poundes Bert, Soonover, f f
Perpenbrink Chas, Fort **Wayne, f f**
Pickens Nettie, Belle **Union, f f**
Pierce J W, Peru, f f
Pace B T, Salem, f f
Pierce E A, Indianapolis, f f
Pierce E A & Burt, Indianapolis **f f**
Parr Enoch, Harristown, f f
Page W D, Fort Wayne, f f
Page A D, Fort Wayne, f f
Pinkerton C D, Huntington, **leg & game**
R, progle L W, Monticello, **lang**
Rand W M, Franklin, f f
Rogers E C, Greentown, **l br**
Ridge R W, Brownsville, **f f**
Richards S L, Mt Zion, f f
Robinson C A, Gwynneville, f f
Rockwell Wm, Brookville, f f
Rockafellar R J, Brooksville, f f
Robinson C A, **Morristown, l br, p r, lang,**
etc
Smoker John, Goshen, lang
Searls E D, Elkhart, f f
Sheffer W K, Kendallville, f f
Stalker E J, Bedford, red caps
Stoner D A, Rensselaer, turkeys, **ducks,**
gee e
Stanley J T, Westfield, f f
Schwegman Geo C, Richmond, g
Seeger Geo Jr, La Fayette, houdans
Servies J H, New Market, w c
Strop E S, Angola, lang, **etc**
Schrank D, Preble, f f
Schifield W A, Howlands, f f
Silver & Brown, Pendleton, f f
Stridham Lillie, Fountain City, **f f**
Schrank Dayton, Preble, f f
Twells & Scottens, Montmorenci, red caps
Totan Wm, Indianapolis, leg
Twells R, Montmorenci, p r, br, etc
Tutewiler, H D, Indianapolis, bantams
Upson E H, Wilmont, f f
Vanseyoc John H, Arlington, p r
Van Matre A P, Yorktown, l br, **wy**
Williamson E R, Waterloo, ham
Warren Albert, K, Lebanon, m, i g
Wintz J A, Morris, w c b polish
Woods N E, Pecksburg, l bra, p r
Williams G M, Monroeville, w p r
White W P, Rushville, p r, etc
Wood N E, Plainfield, f f
Wood N E, Pecksburg, f f
Wilson H A, Medora, f f
Wheeler C L, Nobleville, f f
Wa son Chas T, Rockfield, f f
Wade Eva, Danville, f f
Young A M, New Albany, g f

Zuck I N, **Waynetown, f f**

IOWA.

Armstrong Harry, Mystic, br & **p r**
Appleton J W, Odebolt, wy, leg
Axline W H, Harlan, l br
Basley Wm H, Anita, ham, leg
Brott S, Atlantic, ham
Best & Frazier, Atlantic, **lang**
Ball A M, **Ames,** lang
Beale E M, **Grundy** Centre, lang
Bigley H **A L,** Langworthy, f f
Burrier **Iowa H,** Farmington, f f
Bailey Phil, **West Liberty,** f f
Baldwin **Fred E, Des** Moines, f f
Blake Mary E, Columbus Junction, f f
Bollman A M, Lenox, l br
Bancroft Jos, **Cedar** Falls, b p r, j bao
Busted Mrs W, Red Oak, l c lang
Baxter H, Webster City, red caps
Bowen W O, Pleasant Plain, b p
Brown Geo, Paulina, f f
Brayden A L, Northfield, p r, wy
Blackburn Chas, Lamont, red caps
Baxter H, Webster City, red caps
Brown M T, 1208 Grand Ave, Davenport, f f
Beatty **James, Thornburg,** f f
Bowyer E G, **Algona,** w wy, & p r
Bloom Wm, **De Witt,** lang
Benton E D, **Creston,** b turkeys
Clark W L, Jessup, b lang
Cameron Mrs M J, Hesper, hou, lang, etc
Contant J B, Lette, l br, s & w wy
Caldwell Mrs A M & Son, Iowa **Falls, p d**
Childs B F, Shellsburg, wy
Crane Chas, Parkersburg, f f
Cole F C, Thurman, w p r, etc
Converse S A, Cresco, bronze turkeys
Coughlin Mrs C C, Eldora, f f
Cochrain W E, Corning,
Campbell Ed, West Des Moines, f f
Clements W F, Agency, l br
Dailey Mrs John, Mason City, f f
Duncan John H, Lineville, f f
Danskin Jas, Colo, f f
Donnell J H, **Chanton, g wy**
DeLong Mrs E, **Dows,** geese
Estlack E J, **Sioux City,** p c
Enterprise **Poultry Yards, Beacon, wy,**
p r, etc
Edwards E E, Redding, f f
Elkworth Lalla, Forest City, **b turkeys**
Edson **John T,** Blaine, f f
Eveland Samuel, Rinbeck, s wy
Earl Gus, Anita, leg, p r, wy
Fritz Mrs K M, Arcadia, p r, c
Foreman Chas, Independence, l b
Folren J J, Amanda, l br
Fanett Willis, West Branch, w p r
Flint Jos L, Marion, b p r, wy, p c
Frotman J H, Morning Sun, l br
Flanders C F, Phebolt
Griswold Mrs M M, Clemons, w wy
Gilchrist J M, Odebolt, f f
Gaghagen J W, Eldridge, holland turkeys
George F W, New Hampton, f f
Green H B, Inwood, w wy
Grim C M, Clear Lake, p g
Graves Hattie M, Early, f f
Holt J M, Marshalton, b p r
Howerton Cynthia, Lynnville, f f
Hollenbeck Bros, Storm Lake, g wy

IMPROVED
Excelsior
Incubator

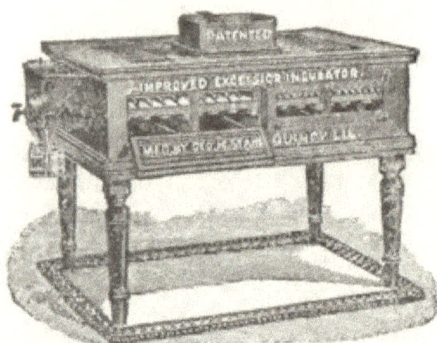

Simple, Perfect, Self-Regulating.

HUNDREDS IN SUCCESSFUL OPERATION!

Guaranteed to Hatch Larger Percentage of Fertile Eggs
at less cost than any other hatcher.

Send six cents for Illustrated Catalogue.
Circulars Free.

GEO. H. STAHL,
PATENTEE AND SOLE MANUFACTURER,
Quincy, Ill.

Hers F W, Odebolt, b c
Howie J E, Bloomfield, f f
Halley J N, Nevada, f f
Heller Simon, Ladna, f f
Hamilton W E, Odebolt, f f
Howard J E & Co, Forest City, 1 br
Hanley Jas, Knoxville, f f
Hertzler A F, Burlington, g wy
Holt J P, Marshaltown, b p r
Hayden Z E, Forest City, s c br leg
Holden Mrs Ella, Patterson, f f
Hamilton Wm, Bristow, f f
Hardin John P, Ainsworth, f f
Heverly J J, Center Point, wy, turkeys
Ingram J M, Nevada, f f
Jonrnal N P, Cedar Rapids, f f
Jenkins E S & W L, Gunnell, w p r
Keichner Fred, Nichols, wy
Kooser Mrs S H, Cedar Rapids, buff c
Kegley T J, Ames, b turkeys
King Geo, High Point, s c b leg
Kennedy B F, Andobon, f f
Kranz Geo, Muscatine, s l & w wy, etc
Kelley C H, Breemer, l br
Knapp W F, Forest City, b p r
Kirchner Fred, Nichols, wv
Keer John, Cedar Falls, l br
Lackore E O, Forest City, w c
Limback Henry, Garnaville, l br, etc
Lown F P, Jessup, l br, b p r, etc
Lowenstein Geo, Keoknlk, f f
Leaver S K, Dows, f f
Lorick J J, Jr, Iowa City
Lathrop J H, Oxford Junction, f f
Laughlin W K, Fort Dodge, l br
Lester Frank, Custom, s c b leg, b p r,
Lattig H S, Anita, wy
Mann B E, Des Moines, f f
Miller W H, Independence, b w r
Mosher Mrs Nettie D, West Liberty, p r
McCormie J E, Calmar, b b r g
McErven J H, Marietta, leg
McConwell Charles, Irwin, w & b lang
Mills J M, Bedford, l br, s c w & b leg
McEaniry John, Burlington, m & p ducks
Morgan F A, Cedar Rapids, wy
Murphy Robert W, Malcome, f f
Marshall Gregory, Cresco, f f
Minteer J A, Conrad Grove, p r, p d, etc
Mills S B, Ames, Hamburg
Mesara Mat, Boonesboro, b c, br, ducks
Montague L W, Center Junction, l br
Newcomb P, Cedar Rapids, p g
Norris G S, Creston, b b r pile p g
Neal T M, Bristow, b lang, s l wy
Ochiltree Thos J, Morning Sun, f f
Oaklawn Poultry Yards, Shellsburg, r c, p r, etc
Osgood G W, Casey, f f
Ochiltree Thos J, Morning Sun
Ormshee T, Muscatine, f f
Parker John M, Independence, f f
Penn J A, White Pigeon, l br, etc
Pitzer Mrs E W, Hillsdale, p r, c, etc
Pitman J M, Coin, f f
Pickerill G N, Bunnells, f f
Peterson E J G, Davenport, f l
Pierce M A, Corning, w leg
Pinkerton A, Shambaugh
Pease C C, Stuart, p b turkeys
Pfander J W, Clarinda, g & s wl y, etc

Pier J W, Dubuque, f f, pig, parrots
Parker John M, Independence, lang
Rice Leonard, Davenport, wy
Richardson J W, Nugent, br, c, etc
Rowe H E, Schaller, br & turkeys
Ruff Peter, Burlington, leg
Richard Martin, Grunnell, b turkeys
Rigg T F, Sioux City, r c b leg
Russell M S, Bayard, f f
Reed M B, M D, Cromwell, f f
Smith Mrs M A, Gilman, lang
Schreiber J W, Aplington, f f
Streby H L, Vail, g wy, b p r
Scott Geo A, Wadena, f f
Sargent Bert, Richland, p r
Shomp O, Bradford, Ham, leg, br, etc
Secor E E, Forest City, b c, blk m, etc
Smith Mrs W T, Redding, f f
Sober Mrs Isabel, Farragut, l f
Stanley Morris, Springville, br, p r
Thomason H O, Storm Lake, red caps
Triller Chas S, cor Main & Fourth St, Lyons, lang
Thiem E O, Vail g wy
Todd J L, Atlantic, f f
Thompson Bros, Coming, l br
Todt Adolph, Wilton Junction, b p r, etc
Thompson J P, Forest City, buff c
Tinker E J, De Witt, lang
Todd J L, Atlantic p r, wy
Udall C H, Jessup, leg, p r, etc
Vannoy A M, Hedrick, l br, wh m
Wilkinson R B, Seymour, Houdans
Walter A F, Odebolt, Peacomb p r
Warner A B, Harlan, buff c
Wagner C B, Albia, b p r
Wilbur G L, Glad Brook
Wolf Mrs Blair, West Branch, l br
Williams J E, Des Moines, f f
Winster John, Keokuk, wy
Wine P D, Amelia, w lang & w p r
Yegge M F, DeWitt, g b, dork

ILLINOIS.
Austin Mrs Eliza, Shunway, f f
Axtey H V, Merrimack Point, f f
Ashey Albert, Ridott, f f
Abbott Mrs S C, Mahomet, buff c
Alphonso E, Washington, birds
Aldrich Mrs D A, Millington, s l wy, etc
Andrews C H, Buckley, w e
Anderson Mrs W E P, Carlinville, l br
Barton E M, Hinsdale, lang
Banewolt H M, Peoria, s c b leg
Bartholomew & McCory, Decatur, l b
Brownback J M, Blue Mound, b c
Baird L & Co, Eureka, l br, w & b c
Birnstill C Gustave, Lockport, f f
Ballard Dr H F, Chens, p e
Basters Geo, Oak Park, hou
Bast E E, 1328 Dunning St, Chicago, br leg
Bewell F L, Evanston, lang
Brown Charles W, North Peoria, g
Bartlett W A, Jacksonville, f f
Bratt W N, Washington, wy
Browning G W, Lincoln, b sumatras
Bloomingdale M, Shabbona Grove, b p r
Burton J W, Hinsdale, p r, c, etc
Ballentine Walter, Argenta, blk c
Burton & Ulam, Rock Island, f f
Baldwin Jay, Abingdon, f f
Burton J W, Peoria, f f

Bender J, Canal Fulton, p r, br leg, etc
Burke A J, Elm Grove, f f
Bunsen P J, & Bros, Shiloh, p g, etc
Clayton Martha, Saline Mines, f f
Corpe Mrs M A, Colfax, f f
Corzine J F, Jerseyville, f f
Cooch Frank, Camargo, f f
Crachel James, Browns, f f
Cummings D, Essex, f f
Carter L J, Aledo, b p r
Corrington W M, Prentice, p r, l br, etc
Clark A A, Milroy, r c b leg
Cross C V, Peoria, b c, l b
Colton J W, Princeton, i g
Churchman C F, Decatur, f f
Chipman W F, MtCarmel
Cambell W S, Streator, l br
Cropper Robert, Warren, r & s c br leg
Constant John E, Buffalo Hart, p r
Cockhill C H, Perry, w & b leg, lang, etc
Cleave W H, Buckley, p c
Camphee Wm T, Streator, f f
Chesher P D, Bloomingdale, f f
Cook E H, Union, bra, leg, ducks, tur, etc
Duff C Lester, Clay City, f f
Doyle Alfred, 45 Market St, Chicago, l & d br
Drake Geo T, Bethel, p r
Dawkins W H, Pan, f f
Davison Ferdie, Alvin, f f
De Forest Frank, Cissna Park, f f
Davis L C, Emery, f f
Dawdy J W, Abingdon, f f
Eckert H C, Belleville, lang, s c wy, leg, etc
Edson M L, Jacksonville, b p r, b e
Ferguson H L, Blue Mound, p c
Fisher R R, McConnell, w b & p c, p r, s & w wy
Fick P D, Dwight, f f
Flint S F, Peoria, p r & s wy
Fry R T, Olney, f f
Foot J B, Norwood Park, l b, p r, p c, etc
Fox F X, Belleville, b c
Ford M E, Illiopolis, f f
Field Fanny, Chicago, f f
Gaddis Mrs John Wayne City, f f
Gelvin E L, Duncan, b p r, etc
Gerhart R H, Allison, f f
Gleason R Ellen, Forest, f f
Girtman Cora, MtPulaski, f f
Grubb Guy, Rushville, wh p r, etc
Gregory Ira, Lexington, p r
Golliday F P, Joliet, lang
Goss Ligel F, Atwood, l br
Grant B S, Tonica, f f
Gelder F A, Palmyra, lang
Gearing J M, Upper Alton, f f
Grimes A M, Pittsfield, p g
Grundy Fred, Morrisonville, f f
Gifford M B, Buckley, wh lang
Gephart H O, 215 Artesian Ave, Chicago
Going Fred, Okawville, f f
Gaddis Jake H, Wayne City, f f
Huntley S J, Springfield, f f
Hutchinson W S, Nunda, f f
Hughey Etta, Abingdon, f f
Huber Sam, Charleston, f f
Hays S J, Graid, f f
Hilton Wm E, Rock Island, f f
Hughes John, Table Grove, b c

Heimlich D F, Jacksonville, f f
Hickman Harry A, Vandalia, f f
Harding Carrie, Scottsville, f f
Hawkins C B, Pleasant Plains, f f
Hallcock J H, Bradford, f f
Hammer A, Rose Hill, f f
Hinds S A, Reduun, f f
Hogle W W, South Evanston, f f
Hunt H C, San Jose, s c w leg, s s ham, p r, etc
Harper C C, Mt Carmel, lang
Humphrey A G, Henry, d br
Hantz J J, 1361 W Harrison St, Chicago, b p r
Havenhill Mabel, Newark, b p r & b tur
Hornbeck E S, Winchester, w,p r, b t
Heuse Mrs John, Hersman, f f
Holloway Oscar, Wing, Liv Co, f f
Hortenstine Mrs John B, Mattoon, f f
Hizer C A, Rochelle, p c, hog, etc
Icom John, Stronghurst, l br, lang, etc
Jones David, Wyoming, f f
Jackson John A, Winnebago, s l wy
Jordan F, 3142 Groveland St, Chicago, f f
Jones Jas E, Green Valley, p d, b pr, etc
Kelley & Summers, Curran, f f
Kirchgraber J Jr, Mattoon, l br
Kent Geo B, Kewanee, r c br leg
Keene L A, Van Buren, tur, wy, ducks
Kendall F R, Byron, f f
Knowles W H, La Crosse, f f
Laybold Mrs L, Chusman, f f
Longshore Mrs M, Cambridge, f f
Lewis Albert, Ohio, f f
Luhosen & Craven, Ladorns, b lang
Lowe Johnson, 6208 Sangamon St, Englewood, f f
Lampson J R, Chapin, b p r
Millar J T, Williamsville, b c
Muchlenfield Henry, Quincy, g wy, hon, etc
Mallery Geo L, Barry, w wy, etc
McCracken D P, Paxton, f f
Munger F M, DeKalf, f f
McNutt D W, Washington, f f
Mann A H, Eldena, b p r
Moxley C A, Rosemond, b p r
McKinley Geo M, Paris, s d g
Milk C & A, Mt Palatine, r, lang, p d
McNay J W, Duncan, p r
McKenzie J L, Champaign, l br, lang, etc
Morgan A, Royal, f f
Meitchell R B & Co, Chicago, f f
Mortimer J T, Pan-Pan, f f
Mundy C K, Belvidere, f f
Moore C, Roanoke, f f
Milton J Romine Irving, f f
Nelson Wm, Galva, f f
Norris Will T, Tallula, f f
Nisbet Mrs James, Rollo, f f
Norton Mrs M J, Ashley, f f
Noble M B, Otterville, s c b leg, b tur
Newbern Jno W, Mt Palatine, b t, p ducks
Nettle R T, Peoria, lang
Nevins Bros, Modesto, b r r, s c b leg
Noyes W W, Lyndon, b p r, g bantams
Ornellas John, Springfield, f pig, g pigs
Ormsbee T, Chicago, f f
Omsted L A, Elburn, f f
Oaten Mrs Vannie, Vermon, l, d br
Owen Horace, Plano, f f

Pitkin Geo T, 3438 Rhodes Ave, Chicago, f f
Perry Dwight J, Earlville, b p r, dk br
Phillips W A, 18 Congress Park, Chicago, f f
Pfingston J E, Odell, d br
Pratt Geo W, Wauconda, 1 wy
Pettet Geo A, Kewanee, w p r, w wy, etc
Pantenney M A, Butler, b c
Root Morris E, Chillicothe, s e w leg
Retting F, DeKalk, f f
Rucker Bros, Literberry, b & w turkeys
Ryuearston E, Brimfield, p r & s wy
Rhodes John F, Toulu, f f
Rogers B H, Ravenswood, r c b leg
Robertson Dan, Palmyra, b c
Rowe E A, Cameron, s e br leg
Robinson & King, Sandwich, r c b leg, wy, etc
Renfro S W, Collinsville, l br
Rucker J R, Literberry, w p r
Rosswer Louis, Blue Island, f f
Rippey Rev G W, Atwood, f f
Ross D H, Kansas, f f
Rogers B E, Lake Bluff, p r & b w leg
Shoemaker Bros, Freidhort, f f
Smith Mrs R N, Chebanse, f f
Sells W T, New Bedford, f f
Smith Byron E, Newman, f f
Stout Joe, Dana, f f
Sword G W, Lanark, f f
Soper O F, Stillman Valley, f f
Stahl Geo H, Quincy, f f
Sewell F L, Evanson, f f
Steward Harry, Atwood, red caps
Stuart Mrs Norwood, f f
Spalding T B, Edwardsville
Schiffer W K, Waterloo, f f
Sylvester Geo E & Son, Peoria, l br
Smith Ed, Peoria, p r, w leg, coch, wy, etc
Springer Bros, Springfield, l br
Shelton Rev J N, Petersburg, s e w leg
Small E A, Elburn, f f
Steep Ed, Morris, l & d br, & p bantams
Savill Bros, Canton, s e w & b leg
Smith Miss Luella M, Ohio, l b
Search H M, Mackinaw, f f
Snyder D M, Abingdon,
Snyder Nell A, Elmwood, f f
Syder Carl, Elmwood, f f
Shoemaker J S, Dakota, f f
Thomas John, Strawn, p c
Taylor F H, Foosland, l br
Tucker Mrs Wm, Colfax, f f
Thurston A, Brownstown, f f
Thompson H P, Flanagan, f f
Tibbetts Henry, Neponset, p r
Ticklin A C, Charleston, f f
Thornton Grant, Sadoms, f f
Van Doren W H, Buckingham, l br
Volans G, Irving Park, f f
Walker Chas A, Maquon, p r
Wingate L A, Blue Island, f f
White James E, Eaglewood, w p r
Welch S O, Hineshow, f f
White D G, Rock Island, g & b wy
Winchester S H, Elmore, wy, p r
Wittstown Wm & Bro, Peoria, b & s e w leg
Wenige L G, Belleville, pug, f f
Wertzler A, Downer's Grove, p c
Wise John M, Freeport, hou & lang
Wood J O, Friendsville, l br

Yoder J J, Arthur, b p r
Young Mrs W E, Macompin

IRELAND.

Cooper J C, Cooper Hill Lenreick, f f

KANSAS.

Alexander J D, Wichita, f f
Ames E R, Fairfield, f f
Andrews M L, Arkansas City, wy, bantam
Anno Emma M, Colony, f f
Ames G S, Fairfield, f f
Bird W R D, Emporia, wy
Brosins Emma, Topeka, l br, tur
Barton A W, Abilene, leg, wy, dom
Bashor A S, Salina, f f
Bartlett L J, Osawatomie, f f
Blanton John, Armordale, f f
Bonebrake E A, Abidena, red caps, lang, coch
Brendsley W L, Ottawa, g f
Burdick S C, Clay Center, lang, coch, etc
Barier, Eureka, f f
Becker F A & Co, Wichita, f f
Blair Geo A, Ashland, f f
Bayless D T, Winfield, f f
Broadstone, H W, Paris, f f
Blair E A, Whitney, f f
Beatan Wm, Newton, f f
Black W R, Augusta, f f
Bird W W, Bluff City, f f
Crum Geo L, Garnett, f f
Cochran A, Olatie, f f
Cobb E N, Frankfort, leg
Childester M, Concordia, min
Croco P C, Winfield, f f
Clark W H, Akron, f f
Carter W F, Clay Center, p g
Conner W G, Labette City, Ferrets
Cazard D W Lacygne, f f
Duker W A, Dukersville, lang
Dey J S, Wellington, lang, tur, ducks
Drake R G, Severance, wy
Drake E R, Cicero, p r, lang, coch, ban, leg
Dille A B, Mrs Edgerton, p r, lang, wy, etc
Douglas J R, Concordia, f f
Dry J S, Wellington, f f
Dubbs W B, Lost Spring, f f
Dickenson & Lockard, Toronto, f f
Dave Mrs Tom, Gardner, l br, leg, lang, etc
Diven DeWitt O, Topeka, lang
Diven DeWitt O, Emporia, f f
Diven O Q, Emporia, f f
Daslow Mrs, M, Topeka, f f
Delong E J, Emporia, f f
Diven G Derriett, Emporia, lang
Darlington, E D, Fordbook, lang
Etlinger Edwin, Griard, f f
Evans Chas, J, Ellsworth, f f
Elledge E P, Arkansas City, f f
Elliot James, Enterprise, bra, etc
Edwards Perry, Emporia f f
Edrington J F, Zyba, f f
Fuller l H, Douglas, f f
Flora E E, Wellington, f f
Farmer W H, Nickerson, f f
Fish Seth, Arkansas City, f f
Faler H G, Wichita, f f
Grizzell E H, Claflin, f f
Groom J P, Wilmot, f f

19

Gallaway C A, Broken Bow, f f	Nyer N R, Leavenworth, f f
Goune Thos E, Ellsworth, f f	Norris Gail, Ottawa, f f
Garitt H E, Topeka, pol	Osborne Louis A, Storton p r, bra, wy, etc
Howell J, Topeka, f f	Orand J W, New Salem, f f
Hatch Mrs L E, Topeka, f f	Owen Thomas, Topeka, wy
Hannon John, Topeka, f f	Owen & Co, Topeka, f f
Hile J W, Valley Falls, f f	Putman Mrs H C, Emporia, lang
Hasfield Edwin, Topeka, f f	Phillips B F, La Cygne, f f
Havett J C, Topeka, f f	Pixley L E, Emporia, f f
Hitchcock F W, Greenleaf, p r	Parks James J, Wichita, lang
Haslet E A, Atchinson, i g	Parsons Dencie I, Brookvill, f f
Holdemess E J, Ellsworth, w wy	Perry C D, Englewood, f f
Hodge M L, Abilene, br, leg	Powell J C, Constant, f f
Hackley Ernest, Ceder Vale, f f	Pabst Wm, Beloit, f f
Hendrick J W, Dorrance, f f	Poister Wm, Enterprise, red caps, lang, ban
Haslett E A, Atchinson, f f	Roberts C A, Winfield, f f
Hawes C D, Gxford, f f	Reheson N H, Emporia, red caps
Hewitt Jno G, Topeka, f f	Rhodes C H, Topeka, f f
Heinsohn Wm, Dundee, Barton, Co, f f	Robinson S S, Hazelton, f f
Hicks C A & Co, Clearfield, f f	Rock Jesse F, Mansato, f f
Hartman P D, Marysville, p r, lang, hou, etc	Roselawn Poultry Yards, Topeka, tum, bra
Haman John, Topeka, wy, pig	Steward A M, Kincaid, f f
Hurlbert Dan'l B, Stockton, p r, ham	Shannon I H, Girard, p r, bra, etc
Hossfeld Ed, Topeka, p g	Sidler A, Lane, bra, coch, lang, etc
Haward W A, Clay Center, f f	Smith M V, Clay Center, ham, p r, etc
Holmes Mrs E C, Windom, f f	Shull Harvey, Topeka, leg
Harcourt G A, Rock, f f	Smith C C, Manhattan, leg
Hunt Gus, Constant, f f	Sparks C A, No Topeka, leg p r
Hammond E D, Junction City, f f	Staatz W H, Enterprise, red caps, p r, etc
Irwin C M, Whichita, br, bro, leg	Snyder John C, Constant, p r, lang, bra
Ingersoll F F, Kensington, f f	Shrrtz Aaron, No Topeka, br, p r, etc
Jones G W, Whichita, f f	Snyder D A, Wichita, leg, p r, wy
Kinzey A F, Douglas, br, coch, leg, etc	Scott John, Wichita, coch
Lucas J P, Topeka, f f	Sproul Belle L, Frankfort, leg
Kerns W D, Baldwin, span leg, ham	Schoff H W, Wichita, f f
Keagy M B, Wellington, p r, leg	Smith Wm R, Wichita, f f
Kellogg, & Alexander, Wichita, l g	Showalter A I, Halstead, f f
Kidder R E, Topeka, f f	Saatz W H, Enterprise, f f
Kirkpatrick M M, Conver, f f	Smith L D, Greenleaf, f f
Kimball Chas M, Neodesha, f f	Skinner O E, Clombus, f f
Kincaid C E, Portland, Summer Co, f f	Snoke D T, Wichita, f f
Lenbert S H & Co, Nevarre, leg	Stemberg Theodore, Ellsworth, coch
Larrabee F H, Hutchinson br, wy	Sherrard D S, Winfield, f f
Lawyer R M, Genola, f f	Shannon Walter, Tisdale, f f
Lorton W R, Rock, f f	Shearer W H, Arkansas City, f f
Litzke A H, Junction City, f f	Spitler S S, Maize, f f
Landon J B, Russell, f f	Stevens Ed W, Kechi, f f
Love Mrs Geo, Arkansas City, f f	Steel Wm Benden, f f
Monfort W F, Concordia, f f	Sharks C A, No Topeka, f f
Martin Henry, Canton, ham	Shaw Wilson, Constant, f f
Mulkey C T, Wichita, p coch, p r	Smith W H, Raymond, f f
McMiller R H, Chapman, f f	Tripp Mrs A S, Winfield, f f
Myers Henry, Topeka, f f	Tucker, A J, Onrida, f f
McCreary J A, Emporia, leg	Tibbitts Edward J, Atchison, f f
Munsell Mrs G A, Wichita, leg	Thomas H A, Scranton, coch
McGrew S B, Holton, wy, leg, etc	Treat C S, Wichita, coch, p r
Measer J J, Hutchinson, f f	Tharpe & White, Emporia, f f
Mercer Ulcey, Concordia, f f	Topping C V, Enterprise, f f
Murcay John A, Arkansas City, f f	Thompson A, Seely, f f
Mayer Henry, Topeka, g f	Tunnell L B, McPhuson, f f
Myers Bert E, Wellington, lang, tur, ducks	Unthank Jno H, Elm City, f f
Mason J A, Mound Valley, f f	Vesper F H & Son, Topeka, p r, etc
May D M, Emporia, wy	Vanbuskirk Mrs N, Blue Mound, br,
Mabie A H, Yates Center, f f	Volker A, Winona, f f
Moore Frank, Tisdale, f f	Wade Mattie, Fall River, f f
Murrie Chas L, Wichita, f f	Whitright Jos, Canton, f f
McLellan F W, Winfield, f f	Worley J L, Aidlene, f f
McDowell John A, Robinson, f f	Woodhead Mrs, G M, McLouth, f f
Marshall H G, Mead Center, f f	Wattles H A, Bayneville, p r, leg, wy
Mabie A H, Yates Center, f f	
Nipp J B, Winfield, f f	

IMPROVED
Excelsior
Incubator

Simple, Perfect, Self-Regulating.

HUNDREDS IN SUCCESSFUL OPERATION!

Guaranteed to Hatch Larger Percentage of Fertile Eggs at less cost than any other hatcher.

Send six cents for Illustrated Catalogue Circulars Free.

GEO. H. STAHL,

PATENTEE AND SOLE MANUFACTURER,

Quincy, Ill.

Watkins G C, Hiawatha, f f
Weick Carl J, Ellsworth, blk span
Ward Bros, Oneida, leg
Werner J W & Son, Greenleaf, br
Wilson A N, Arkansas, f f
Winfield & Co, Abaline, f f
Winchester, S H, Elmore, f f
Williams G B, Pacola, f f
Workman W J, Ashland, f f
Walter Mrs Samuel, Courtland, f f
Wilcox Harry, Newton, f f
Watkins F L, Harper, f f
Williams Della, Dexter, f f
Walkey C T, Wichita, f f
Young Esther A, Topeka, f f
Yowell J W, McPherson, f f
Young Clarence F, Topeka, f f
Yost Jacob, Topeka, f f

KENTUCKY

Barbee W B, Millersburg, tur
Ballard W H, Shelbyville, tur
Beyer John C, Paduch, l br, hou, leg, etc
Crosby W B, Owensboro, p r, wy, lang
Chadres Jno R, So Canollton, f f
Dickens S B, Hopkinsville, lang
Dutschke W H, Lodiburg, p g
Fleming John M, Augusta, lang
Frymere J B, Preston, p g, ham, etc
Foster John P, Hartford, p r
Gleichman E H, Paducah, g f
Hayeraft D C, Elizabethtown, g f
Ham Mathew E, Julian, f f
Kenney C A, Paris, p g
Kinkead Shelby, Lexington, f f
Macquithy M, Kings Hill, f f
Norris M F, Lexington, f f
Sutton J J, Falmouth, f f
Z—— Jacob Jr, Henderson, l br, w wy, etc

LOUISIANA

Clark Harvy H, New Orleans, lang
Edwards J F, Haughton, g f
Fitch Everett, Haughton, pig
Garig W W, Baton Rouge, f f
Murphy J H, Slidell, g wy
Shaw A E, New Orleans, f f
Sentell G W & Co, New Orleans, f f
Webb G Y, Jr, Minden, p g

LONG ISLAND, NEW YORK.

Geylor F W, Quogue, f f
Homan Elmer E, r c b leg, etc
Seaman Robert, Jericho, f f
Underhill F T, Oyster Bay, f f

MICHIGAN.

Anderson R W, Detroit, leg
Aldrich C P, Battle Creek, w p r
Adams Chas P, Grand Rapids, g f
Bartlett O E, Pontiac, f f
Bement E & Son, Lansing, f f
Barnes Geo S, Battle Creek, f f
Beadle H A, Climax, s wy
Ball J, Marshall, w wy
Belden E E, Battle Creek, b c
Babcock J A, Battle Creek, blk leg
Briggs C A, Onited, i g
Brown F H, Blissfield, f f
Badeau W A, New Haven, lang
Brown B W, Blissfield, lang
Cornell C F, Grand Blanc, f f
Clark J B, Muskegon, b c

Chamberlain Allie, Decatur, f f
Crosby H R, Bichland, w wy
Carrol M, Onondaga, p r
Cummings, R A, Washington, g f
Clement J J, So Haven, w p r
Denson B F, Morence, f f
Dean D C, Adrian, f f
Durkee W S, Paw Paw, w c
Dudley C C, Alba, lang
Dean Artie J, Jr, Adrain, f f
Ecker Frank R, Lowell, w leg
Forker R C, Battle Creek, w leg
Garett Will C, Frontier, f f
Grosvenor E O, Monroe, f f
Grimes F P, Battle Creek, f f
Goss L D, Monroe, p r, s wy
Grimes F F, Paw Paw, blk min
Gandy Geo M, Ypsalanti, p r
Grimes E P, Kalamazoo, p r
Graitot Poultry Yards, St Louis, wy, etc
Howes F H, Itinaca, Gratiot Co, f f
Hurd Mark, Marshall, f f
Hines N E, Charlotte, p c, p r
Hills H S, Ithaca, g f
Hang Edmund, Battle Creek b p r
Haug E, Detroit, w p r
Heffon F C, Battle Creek, w p r
Haynes J H, Decatur, s wy
Hayne C L, Battle Creek, d bra
Henry F C, St Louis, i g
Hartring Geo E, Homer, f f
Hogue C L, Battle Creek, f f
Hang Edmund, Dearbon, w & b, p r
Jones C W, Bichland, s wy
Jenks Mary, Denton, f f
Judkins F G, Battle Creek, ban
Kilby E J, Marshall, w c
Knapp E W, Galesburg, dom
Kshpaugh J L & Co, Clinton, b c
Krull Jno C, Three Rivers, f f
Lawrence W J, Battle Creek, tur
Look G, Lowell, ham
Lamb C A, Grand Rapids, g f
Lachlan D P M, York, Brown leg
Luther Jas H, Lamont, f f
Mugg E, Dundee, l bra
Marlhoof W E, Galesburg, f f
McVarney J B, Battle Creek, f f
Mead A F, Edwardsburg, red caps
McCall Ray, Ithaca, g f
McCann James, Ypsalanti, g f
Michigan Poultry Farm, Saline, f f
Myers A W, Gobleville, w wy, b p r
Nissly Geo J, Salina, l br
Nevins N N, St Louis, g f
Nichols A L, Hichong Comers, w c b pol
Oak Lawn Poultry Farm, Ypsalanti, f f
Ohusted H E, Deaton, l br
Oliver W, Battle Creek, g wy
Parker Wm E, Ann Harbor, f f
Prescott N F, Henrietta, f f
Phillips G S, Battle Creek, f f
Pomroy H R, Kalamazoo, red caps
Roseberry Frank, E Saginaw, g f
Rose J, Battle Creek, blk spanish
Richardson G E, Battle Creek, p g
Rice M L, Utica, p c, br, etc
Robinson, W L, Tekonsha, blk min, etc
Richardson Wm, Paw Paw, leg
Slifter S H, Jackson, f f
Segwum Poultry Yards, Lowell lang, w c, etc

Shinner C G, Grass Lake, w p r
Snodgrass M, Battle Creek, p g
Smith M H, Battle Creek, p g
Shanan Bert, Battle Creek, german hares
Schweinforth, N, Jackson, f f
Spear F E, Marquette, leg, w p r
Stolckert Will, Monroe, leg
Strange G, Betyer, bra, etc
Slafer S H, Jackson, f f
Stockwell J B, Clayton, f f
Smith Horace, Lansingburg, f f
Stevens F H, Merrill, f f
Schild Chas, Ionia, s s ham
Thornton F L, E Side Saginaw, f f
Thomas C C, Merrill, f f
The Eureka Poultry Co, Port Huron, f f
Todd Waltz, Ithaca, dom
Torrey A S, Albion, f f
Vieson Fred Detroit, f f
Vosburg A E, Battle Creek, dork
Willis M, Battle Creek, g wy
Ward R H, Marshall, g wy
Worrel E, Battle Creek, p c
Washburn Henry, Battle Creek, w rabbits
Watkins Farms, Detroit, leg
White A A, Tecumseh f f
White C N, Tecumseh, f f
Wadsworth W G, Pittsford, f f
Warren F H, Bay City, f f
Wang John St Louis, f f

MINNESOTA.

Beardsley N S, St Paul, b p r
Bennet Franklin, 315 3rd Ave So Minneapolis, 1 bra
Bohn & Cox, Winona, p r
Blackmore A H, St Paul, b c
Cutler F A, Winona, blk & w wy
Clay J P, Winona, 1 br
Cline Alfred, Delavan, leg, wy, lang
Darby E B, Owatonna, dk br
Deacon & Co, 2 W Third St, St Paul, leg, ducks, guinea f
Everett E L, Minneapolis, wy
Floody P H, 112 East Geranium St, St Paul, p g
Gates Poultry Yards, St Paul, wy
Gaine W H, Stanton, f f
Hiland Delia, St Paul, f f
Holden G D, Owatonna, g wy, etc
Hess & Teet-horn, Winona, wy, javas
Huelster H F, 1091 Reaney St, St Paul, leg, br, bantams
Hancock C L, Chatfield 1 br, wy, ducks,
Johnson A M, Minneapolis, f f
Krier H H, Owatonna, g f
Kling Conrad, Winona, blk pol
Lick Fred, Duluth, f f
Lewis H T, Quincy, f f
Luce C E, Owatonna, b p r
Larson L, Cereal, b p r, geese
Manhattan Park Poultry Ranch, Minneapolis, 1 f
Morisse Geo F, Alexandria, p r
Machum F L, Plainview, f f
Morgan T L, 533 Wabash St, St Paul, 1 br, wy, geese, etc
Miller Gus, Minneiska, p r, wy, etc
Neff W, 345 Waverly Place, St Paul, leg
Nass Wm, Winona, wy, span
Ney B E, 36 Merrill St, St Paul, leg, g
Osmundson John G, Norstrand 1 br

Parlin Leslie, St Paul, b c
Ritt G P, 904 Case St, St Paul, 1 br
Roberts R R & Co, St Paul, wy, leg
Ruen P O, Moland, 1 bra, p r
Smith C D, St Charles, f f
Sherman Geo C, Minneapolis p c
Schultz Wm, 771 Magnolia St, St Paul, wy, p r
Smith Bros, New Brighton, w wy
Tuttle W L, Duluth, f f
Titus S L S, 713 Charles St, St Paul, p r, bra, lang
Vandensen A J, Winona, leg
Wright A N, Gwatonna, wy
Westphal E O, Graceville, f f
Wyandotte & Leghorn Poultry Yards, 223 Arndel St, St Paul
Walstrom Robert, Lake City, bk lang

MISSOURI.

Aul D H, Smithville, f f
Ayer J A, La Plate, i g
Allen N E, Clinton, w p r
Antnin C W, Shell City, f f
Anderson H R, Jakes Prairie, f f
Batkin M M, Japlin, lang
Baker J S W, Millford, f f
Bennett E F, Macon City, f f
Burdaugh Jno, Kiddes, f f
Bagby Willis, Skidmore, p r, w wy
Bryant Fred E, Burlington Junction, lang, wy
Ballard B F, Jr, Raytown, leg, lang
Bothwell Jas, Breckenridge, f f
Cale H L, Clinton, 1 br, lang, p r
Campbell B W, Skidmore, p r, br, etc
Cowles J D, Coloma, lang, ham, tur
Coshow J W, Mechanicsville, s l wy
Darway E J, Urbana, f f
Burrett Aza, Virginia, f f
Doran R F, Bunceton, f f
Dyer R F, Fayetteville, 1 br, lang, p r
Clark C A, Rich Hill, Lang
Emery C A, Carthage, f f
Falkerson F, Lamar, f f
Fry C W, Dunlap, wy, leg, ban
Fant C B, Warrenton, 1 br
Geer Bros, St Mary's, leg, p r, bra
Gaines S A, Onick, f f
Holster Felix, St Mary's, f f
Hazlitt L F, Lamar, f f
Holster Felix St Mary's, f f
Hewes Theodore, Trenton, leg, p r
Heether J A, Huntsville, ban
Hawkins Sallie, Hawkins, p r
Hotchkiss T W, Folona, f f
Hammer Chas, Raytown, Jackson Co, f f
James H W, Monroe City, p r, bra
Koehl F J, Kirksville, 1 br, c
Kendig J D, Burlington Junction, leg
Langenecker Geo, St Louis, leg
Ladd W A, Franklin, f f
Lyerly C C, Sedgewickville, f f
Lindsey J W, East Lynne, f f
Lavin Gus, Warrensburg, b p r
Little J M, Breckenridge, p r, leg
Mackey Bettie Clover, Clarksville, p r, br
Miller Chas G, Boonesville, 1 br, lang
Melville Robert, Hannibal, p r, wy, leg
Mills W, Maitland, b & w c, wy, lang
Mathews J H, Tarkio, wy, 1 br, etc
Menger Geo J, Palmyra, p r

PHILANDER WILLIAMS,

TAUNTON, MASS.

ORIGINATOR OF THE OLD AND RELIABLE

Autocrat Strain of Light Brahmas

LARGEST SIZE!   FINEST FORM!
MOST PERFECT COLOR!

— AND THE —

BEST LAYERS OF ANY STRAIN IN THE WORLD!

DARK BRAHMAS

THAT CANNOT BE EXCELLED.

PARTRIDGE COCHINS.

FASHIONABLE COLOR, BEAUTIFUL PENCILLING.

Barred and White Plymouth Rocks,
Silver Laced Wyandottes,
Gold Laced Seabright Bantams,
Black and Mottled Russian Trumpeter Pigeons,
Yellow Fantail Pigeons.

Eggs for Hatching, $5 for 13; $8 for 26; $10 for 39.

SEND FOR PRICE LIST.

McIntosh J G, Valley Park, f f
McCall D A, Westboro, f f
Petts F H, Norway, tur
Petts N B & Sons, Warsaw, f f
Petty J A, Foster, f f
Palmer Seth, Moberly, l g
Rice J M, Riverdale, f f
Rundell John E, Lamar, lang, p r, pig
Ragsdale, J W, Paris, l bra
Rogers J W, Shipman, wy, lang, p r
Straitfield J, Odessa, l bra
Souther A G, Ferguson, w wy
Streight Elizabeth, Blairstown, f f
Staples W H, Pierce City, f f
Steinmesch Henry, Lutter, p r, wy
Strode Will T, Independence, wy
Sayler, W G, Burnington Junction, leg
Shepherd N J, Eldon, l f
Taylor May, Hale, bra
Taylor A C, Green City, p r, wy, tur
Thompson Adam, Amity, i g
Vogeler L S, Three Mile Prairie, f f
Vandandingham N B, Tarkio, l bra, etc
Walker J S, Centerville, lang
Wale & Rundell, Lamar, bra, p r
Whitney L H, Trenton, leg
Williams J A, Perry, p r, min
Young J E, Gratis, f f

MARYLAND.

Abele John D & Co, 526 Gorsuch Ave, Waverly, Baltimore
Boileans Chas E, Middletown, f f
Brown G O, Baltimore, f f
Beans Howard, Baltimore, blk leg
Bell Wm D, Laytonsville, w wy
Bonman J R, Cockeysville, p r, etc
Bonman Henry H, Hagerstown, f f
Bast E E, Chicago, b l
Bealers Stock Farm, Clifton, lang
Cooper Elbert, Oringo Mills, lang
Crowell J W, Cambridge, lang
Catlin P J, Catlin, f f
Cost John L, Hagerstown, f f
Cramer K T, Frederick, f f
Clopper Jno A, Rohrersville, f f
Davis G W, Pleasantville, i g
Dickey C B, Washington, D C, lang
Crawford H L, Washington, D C, p r
Engel J D, Middleburg, lang
Fick G A, Baltimore, Swallows
Frey W H, Washington, D C, lang
Goldsborough E Y, Frederick, f f
Garlinger B A Jr, Hagerstown, f f
Heirommus H D, Hagerstown, f f
Johnson Wm C, Frederick, f f
Jarrell Chas E, Hillstow, f f
Kemp E Thomas, Frederick, f f
Klemm Chas H, Baltimore, f f
Knox Geo W, Washington, D C, f f
Lehman H F, Hagerstown, i g
Morrison Henry H, Hyattsville, f f
Oha Wm, Waterville, f f
Phillips Wm B, Jessups, w leg, & w min
Pyle John R, Mill Green, f f
Price & Walker, Damascus, f f
Price Littleton E, Damascus, i g, etc
Reifsinder Jesse, Frederick City, f f
Rench Misses, Hagerstown, f f
Rhumbold John, Baltimore, l bra, etc
Rupenacht Ed, Gittings, f f
Schmenner Charles, Baltimore, tum

Sweigart W W, York Road, red caps, etc
Schumd Edward S, Washington, Birds, pig, etc
Taylor Samuel W, Baltimore, pig
Walther F A, Rechord, f f
Wolf W W, Knoxville, f f

MASSACHUSETTS.

Anthony & Fox, Taunton, i g
Aldrich Geo S, Westboro, f f
Attleton E L, Springfield, f f
Atherton W B, Newton Lower Falls, wh fantail pig
Andrews Albert W, 17 Catherine St, Worcester, leg, etc
Austin W, Suffield, f f
Auckland W, Winsted, f f
Aenold J, Springfield, f f
Albee E E, Millville, f f
Abbott Stephen A, Beverly, w wy
Albee E E, Millville, s c br leg, p r
Alderman F E, Adams, blk & bro leg, hou
Auckland Wm, Springfield, w f b span
Attleton E L, Springfield, d br
Ames Hill Poultry Yards, d br
Aitkin William J, Brighton, w leg
Atwood D, Millbury, f f
Avery Mrs F L, E Pepperell, f f
Akerman John O, Newburyport, lang
Bacon Eugene, Nolescot, lang
Ball H S, Shrewsbury, b & w p r
Buckman Geo S, Melrose Highlands, d br
Bruce Chas, Pontoosuc, b leg
Bartlett W H, Hyannis, l br
Bartlett Edw E, Newburyport, s wy
Buffington R G, Fall River, b & b c, etc
Bradley Bros, Lee, p r
Ballou C A, 24 Lee St, Worcester, d br, etc
Beckett C L, Peabody, l br, s c b leg
Barnes J M, Westfield, Hou,
Bartle Poultry Supply Co, Oxford, f f
Burnham Alvin, South Essex, wy & leg
Bright W Ellery, Waltham, br, wy, etc
Benjamin E E, Greenfield, w & s l wy
Baldwin & Tait, Chicopee, f f
Bingham A, Springfield, f f
Binnie Bros, Springfield, f f
Bacon W Frank, Cambridgeport, f f
Bruce C N, Westboro, w & s wy
Benton E B, Waverly, br
Buck Wm H, Webster, hou
Butler J H, So Weymouth, s s ham, g b
Bowker James, So Weymouth, p g
Bachelder C A, Ayer, w wy
Bingham J M, Westboro, l br, w p r
Barton James, So Natick, p r, p c
Bass E A, Brockton, red caps
Bassett Joseph, Yarmouthport, p r, w p r, etc
Bugbee C L, Spencer, f f
Bearse Alton, Hyannis, b c
Besserer I T, Holyoke, lang
Brainard E A, East Hampton, f f
Baker Stanley, Marshfield, l duckwing, g b
Burns T F, Lowell, s l wy, etc
Baker Clement H, So Yarmouth, f f
Baker H S, West Dedham, f f
Brods & Barton, Weston, p r, p c, etc
Butler A W, Brockton, blk ham
Bonney W E, South Hanover, f f

Bumford H H, Waltham, l b
Bucknah Geo C, Melrose Highlands, l br
Burlingham Franklin, East Foxboro, p d
Brown N Porter, Westboro, f f
Bowker Geo H, Waltham, br
Batchelder C A, Ayer, br
Comey E C, Somerville, l b
Cromack G W, Stoneham, l br
Cutting & Estes, Quincy, g
Chapman F W, Melrose
Charles River Poultry Yards, New. Lower Falls
Combs C B, Woods Holl, lang
Carpender Geo H, Griswoldville, f f
Cahoon C L, New Bedford, w wy, b leg, etc
Collamore J B, Springfield, s l wy
Crehore C L, Chicopee, l b
Child Harrison H, East Walpole, w p r & p ducks
Cobb C L, Attleboro, w wy, w p r
Crinier J M, Middleton, l b, c, etc
Cushing W S, So Hingham, f f
Collingwood Fred H, Hebronville, f f
Crocker Fred R, Yarmouthport, f f
Cady Wm C, Southbridge, lang
Carleton John, East Sandwich, l br
Crawford David N, S Weymouth, ban
Curtis Chas F, Stoneham, w leg
Cushing G M, Milton, w p r
Carpenter T J, Worcester, blk & w min
Clark H Manly, Randolph, b wy, l br
Crossley & Clark, No Abington, f f
Calkins A B, Palmer, w wy
Crocker Watson B, East Brewster, p r
Coggeshall Edw H, New Bedford, ban
Callanam J B, Springfield, f f
Carpenter T J, Worcester, f f
Comey Elbridge C, Somerville, l br
Coburn F A P, Lowell, f f
Colton J C, Springfield, f f
Cutler Henry, Newton, f f
Coffin H A, Cummingsville, f f
Carlock Charles T, Cambridgeport, f f
Caleb D C, Roslindale, Boston, f f
Cole Warren M, West Boxford, f f
Callette E S, Spencer, f f
Cromack G W, Stoneham, bra
Downs Wm H, Salem, l br
Down T W, New Bedford, g
Dunham Harry, Nantucket, p r
Dennis J H, Rockport, p r
DeForest A M, Worcester, laced wy
Develley George, So Hanover, p r, ducks & geese
Dean Nathaniel, Holbrook, l br
Dean J H, Quincy Point, p e, r c w leg
Dudley S & Son, Harvard, b lang, etc
Dyer Joshua, Truro, f f
Delano J H, Newburyport, l br
Dalton B W, Franklin, f f
Dougherty M J, Lynn, Lang
Dolbedre Fred T, West Newton, lang
Essex Poultry Yards, Essex, wy
Emery Fred C, Woburn, f f
Edwards I F, Westville, f f
Eastman W H, Stoneham, hou
Emerson Henry E, Quincy, p g
Eldridge Edmund, Yarmouth, p r
Edson Rev Edward, Yarmouthport, p r
Everett G O, Dover, w p r
Fuffs C, Lynn, f f

Fletcher Geo N, Belmont, l b
French H E, Dedham, f f
Fillebrown A A, Ayer, w p r
Flanders Chas S, Springfield, w wy
Foulds Bro, Springfield, w wy
Foster Wm B, Beverly, w leg, & p ducks
Fish Frank L, Taunton, br leg
Farm Poultry, Box 2118, Boston
Field A M, & G L, Taunton, br leg, ban
Foster H R, Ashly, i g
Field C, North Adams, w wy
Faxon C T, Braintree, red caps, l b
Felch I K & Son, Natick, l b, p r, w wy, etc
Feather Geo, Dorchester, eng owls & turbits
Fenton Ira B, Framingham
Fowle Wm R, Chelmsford, w & p r, r c w leg
Felton A C, Orange, f f
Fairfield H, Walpole, ducks
Fillebrown A A, Clinton, f f
Field Fanny, New Salem, f f
Fenton Ira B, Framingham, f f
Frail Wm R, Spencer, s c b leg, b coch, etc
Garland F L, Warnersville, leg
Graves Geo & Son, Amherst, w p r
Gay O B & Son, South Bridge, w p r
Gurney S P, Whitman, b p r
Gibbs R A, Rock, w wy
Gardner A W, Springfield, w wy, blk leg
Glenridge Poultry Yards, Wellesley Hills, br leg
Giddings F E, Van Deusen, blk min
Goodwin W M, Salem, f f
Glidden N A, Chelmsford, f f
Goddard Joseph, Roxbury, p r
Gunnison Miss H M, Amesbury, l br, s c b leg
Griffin M E, Sterling Junction, f f
Gum L B, Lanesboro, p r
Groce Wm R, Rockland, wy
Hutchinson Dr N V, Somerville, br
Holden F E, Tully, f f
Howland E R, Sandwich, f f
Holbrook E A, Winchester, l br & b p ban
Hawkins A C, Lancaster, p r, wy
Heronx A A, Lawrence, pouters
Handy H T, Pocasset, f f
Handy J T, Cataumet, f f
Hopkins & Thomas, Conway, b c, l br, ban
Harris C W, Lynn, f f
Heronx A A, Lawrence, pig
Harrington W W, Wellesley Hills
Howe E A, Brightwood, i g
Henderson Frank T, Boston, p r
Hartford N B, Watertown, leg, wy
Hatch Mrs A G, Springfield, f f
Holbrook G K, Saugus, blk leg
Hopkins L T, Conway, coch
Huckinson Dr N N, No Abington, l br, p e
Hovey M, Sutton Springs, f f
Hanes H L, Springfield, f f
Holmes J B, Kingston, f f
Hurd J S, Orleans, lang
Hollis W A, No Abington, hou
Hubbard J A, Cambridge, l wy
Hunter A F, South Natick, p r, w wy, etc
Holway Mrs Isaac F, West Barnstable, l b, coch
Harris E A, Amherst, b c, & red caps

Hallett Reuben, Yarmouthport, l br
Hudson Robert, Highlandville, red caps
Hallett Fred, Yarmouthport, p r, w p r, w wy
Hancheit J L, Westfied, f f
Harlow A T, Plymouth, blk leg
Howland Dr A A. Worcester, w wy
Hunt H M, Rockland, red caps
Hallett Charles, Yarmouthport, p r
Henderson James T, Boston, w p r, w wy
Huxley A W. Northampton, l b, p r
Hatch Geo R, Springfield dk br
Hunter A F, So Natick, f f
Hall W F, Dedham, t f
Hill W F, Dedham, f f
Hinckley Benj L, Woburn, dk br
Hudson H, Highlandville, l b, red caps
Hamilton Col R J, Springfield, l br
Hill Frank P, Ayer, br
Isola P, Newton Lower Falls, br
Johnson H E, Melrose, f f
Jenney Wm J, Fall River, f f
Jones H A, Worcester, f f
Jepson L A, Adams, g f
Johnson l S & Co, 22 Custom House St, Boston, f f
Jewett W N. New Bedford, bantams
James B F, Springfield, f f
Johnson V P, Winchester, f f
Knapp N A. Plainville, f f
King C Jr, Plainville, f f
Kirby E P. East Chatham, w lang
Kimball Wm T, Natick, f f
Knowles William W. Brewster, p r
Kendall H D, Lowell, dk br, p c,
Kelsey M F, Worcester, s wy
King R H, Springfield, b c, & dk br
Kent G L, Belchertown, l br
Lyons A F S, Greenfield, w wy
Lamphree Charles, No Attleboro, p r
Landers E J, Chatham, f f
Lawrence G G, Leominster, f f
Latham C H, Lancaster, p c
Lillibridge C W, Helsonville, w p r, r c w leg
Lathrop A W, Watertown, g l & w wy
Lowell John, Jr, Chestnut Hill, g & s ham
Loud George T, So Weymouth, f f
Lawrence & Welch, Harvard, p r, wy
Leach L W, Lincoln, s c w leg
Loud Wilton, So Weymouth, f f
Leonard A D, Mansfield, blue fantails
Lloyd Dr, Blackinton, i g, etc
Love Daniel, Auburn, imp stock
Loomis J, Springfield, f f
Lovell G, Worcester, f f
Lowell John,Jr, Chestnut Hill, ham
Marshall Geo W, Taunton, br
Montague C C & Bros, Amherst, p r
Mowry D W, No Wilbraham, dk br
Makin J, Brockton, f f
Mathewson F W, Attleboro, w p r, w wy
Macomber B F. So Easton, f f
Mann F W, Milford, f f
Montague C C. Amherst, f f
McKinstry A W, Chicopee, f f
Macy P S, Jr, New Bedford, lang
Moffitt Decatur, w p r, l br, etc
May H B, Natick, p r, etc
Marston Warren, Yarmouthport, f f
McQueston John, Hadley, w p r
Moore E H, Melrose, l br, w p r, etc

Maple Wood Poultry Yards, Malden, p r etc
McKinstry A W, Chicopee, b span
Mackintosh R S, Jr, Boston
Nye Frank, Barre Plains, lang, p r
Norton E H, Westfield, f f
Norton Henry, West Upton, f f
Newhall D, Conway, Franklin Co, p r
Nickerson L O, Chatham, f f
Newhall & White, Lynn, g wy, leg, etc
Noble Frank L, Silver Lake, ducks, tur, etc
Nye E I. Welfleet, p ducks
Newhall F E, West Roxbury, s c w leg
Nickerson John, Chatham, ducks & l br
Ornellos John, Springfield, pig
Pitman E A, Jr, Marblehead,
Power A L, Norwell, bra
Purinton A J, Lynn, wy
Pease Frank N, Brightwood, leg
Putnam Ernest, West Sutton, w & b leg
Potter W C, Hebronville, f f
Perkins George, Gloucester, lang
Phelps Geo E, Springfield, lang
Phelps W A, So Hadley, red caps
Pixby H N, So Lee, lang
Parkin W H, Taunton, blue andalusians
Pingry F S, Littleton, l br, w p r
Pratt Preston, So Weymouth, l & dk br, g bant
Pratt C A. No Abington, bk coch
Porter T P, Brook Farm, l b w leg
Putnam O J, Leomister, p r, & w p y
Pitman E A, Jr, Marblehead, l br, l wy
Pearson Arthur, No Wilmington, pig
Perkins James E, Stoughton, i g, etc
Power A L, Norwell, f f
Pattison C W, Chicopee, f f
Perry Jos M, Brockton, hou
Perkins W H, Watertown, f f
Parker & Wood, No 49 Market St, Boston, f f
Pope C H, Brockton, blk java & w p r
Prince J, Beverly, lang
Pratt Philander, Belmont, br
Payson J S, Jamaica Plain, pr
Rogers H P, Allston, br
Randall Eugene, Belchertown, br
Ransden E A, Elmwood, w p r
Rogers F D, Monson, w p r, etc
Rannenberg Wm, Shelburne Falls, p r
Rudd W H & Son, 10 Merchants Row, Boston, p r
Rankin Jas, So Easton, p ducks
Ray A E, Amherst, w p r, etc
Rivers W H, Adams, p r
Rand A J, Holyoke, w wy, pigs, etc
Reid W A, New Bedford, pheasants
Ryder Wilson, Yarmouthport, p r & wy
Ryder Thomas, Yarmouthport, p r
Ryder Luther, Yarmouthport, p r
Ray A E, Amherst, p r, etc
Rich Horatio C, Oxford, p r, red caps
Reed Fred, So Weymouth, p g
Ropes Reuben W, Salem, s c w leg
Randall Eugene, Belchertown, l br
Rollins W H, 250 Marlborough St, Boston
Rance John, Beverly, f f
Rutter Jesse M, Lawrence, f f
Robinson, E C, Springfield, f f
Richards C A & C H, Brockton, w coch
Roslette & McFadden, Holyoke, p g

Ryder J E, Wellfeet, p ducks
Rocky Hill Poultry Yards, Avon, f f
Steere Tobias, Millis, f f
Smith Arthur, Conway, w c b polish,
Scott Earl M, No Wilbraham, w wy
Sharp J C & A N, Taunton, b c
Shaw J W, Brockton, 1 br
Sylvester W S, Brockton, blk c
Sanderson E J, Waltham, b c
Stevens Abel F, Wellesley, w p r
Smith Mrs Nellie, Springfield, f f
Stahrer Fred, Lawrence, lop rabbits
Shaylor C H, Lee, b p r
Stevens H M, Newburyport, p c
Steele J W, Adams, g f
Streeter Clarence R, Worcester, f f
Stacy S E, Springfield, f f
Seely & Francis, Bridgeport, f f
Scott E M, North Wilbraham, f f
Shove D P, Fall River, l & dk br, & br leg
Stearns H D, Jeffersonville, f f
Smith Nathan E, Waltham, w & s l wy
Stevens Abel F & Co. Wellesley, p r, wy
Spear J G, Quincy, s c br leg, etc
Searles Frank J, Whitseville, p r
Shaw Joseph W, Brockton, 1 br
Snow I, Truro, 1 br
Sturdy J E, Yarmouth, p r
Schofield James, New Bedford, red caps
Story David L, Beverly, 1 br
Smith & Walker, Lee, wh leg
Sherman Chas H, Waltham, jacobins
Smith Bros, Worcester, s c br leg
Sanderson J H, Hatfield, f f
Stetson John M, Brockton, br
Traill Wm H, Spencer, s c br leg, etc
Thompson Morton S, Middleboro, f f
True M E, Woburn, f f
Thissel H A, Clinton, lang
Treadweel W J, Salem
Tirrel Chas F, Weymouth Centre, f f
Turbey Emanuel J, North Chelmsford,
    red caps
Thompson E F, Turner Falls, red caps
Thacher John G, Yarmouthport, p r
Thacher Frank, Hyannis, p r
Trott C E, Weymouth, p r, g
Thomas Edgar H, Quincy Point, p r
Tuttle C R, Wakefield, 1 wy
Thorpe Thomas, Highlandville, s wy
Tillingham C & V, Waterloo, bk min
    p c
Tripp F G, New Bedford, bantams
Turner L C, W Bridgewater, 1 br
Teeha F, Chelsea, b leg, 1 br
Tirrell Gideon, No Abington, g wy
Terry A B, Brockton, s l wy
Tinkham D G, Rock, g s polish
Thomas & Hopkins, Conway, coch
Upham L J, Webster, g wy, p r, etc
Vining Wm H, Leominster, 1 br, bantams
Wilbur J, Somerset, br
Wardle J F, Jr, Walnut Hill, Dedham
    br
Westcott E, So Framingham, bk leg
Ward & Merriam, Springfield, p r
Whitehead Geo W, Springfield, s l wy
Willis Tremont H, Brockton, w wy
Williams Philander, Taunton, p c, 1 br
Wheeler W J, Worcester, f f
Wade John, Jr, Dedham, 1 br
Wilson W H, Shirley Village, 1 br

Wright H B, South Easton, f f
Whipple J C, Bourne, f f
Westgate Fred M, Malden, f f
Williams P, Taunton, f f
Whiting E S, Plainville, leg
Wood William, Warnerville, p r
Wight D R, Fiskdale, w & b min
Westcott E, So Framingham, b leg
Warren W H, Warren, p r
Wood H M, Springfield, f f
Woodhead J H, Leicester, s c wh leg
Whiting Henry, Rockland, b c
Whittier S, Leominster, 1 wy, r c w leg
Willet C S, Brockton, bk leg
Wright A H, S Weymouth, g ban
Weber J, Wrentham, p d
Warren J G, Auburn, f f
Watson C E, Holyoke, lang
White W A, West Taunton, p r
Washburn M C, Tyngsboro, p r, wy
Wilson W H, Shirley Village, 1 br, w p r
Waldron Ferdinand, Dighton, lang
Wilson Mrs A E. Newburyport, 1 br
Wood F A, Fitchburg, wy
Wheeler C A, Brighton, br
Wyer E F, Woburn, br
Woodman R, 169, High St, Boston, br
Yeaton A B, Stoneham, 1 br, & p r
Young Richard H, Westborough, f f

MAINE.

Bird C A, Rich Hill, lang
Bibbler Will R, Eastport, lang
Banks James H, Freeport, w p r
Brown James L, Sacarrappa, lang
Besse C H, E Jefferson, f f
Booth & Bros, Auburn, f f
Blanchard Dr L J, Dexter, lang
Cook L R, Yarmouthville, r c b leg
Coffin Geo P, Freeport, lang
Domtree Weble, Sheep Hatt, lang
Downs W H, Sebec, f f
Day H C, Auburn, br
Drummond, Mrs H T, Vassalborough, f f
Hayes F H, Dexter, p g
Harris Newton W, Portland, p ducks
Heath Mrs C G, E Newcastle, f f
Hennings John J, Waldoboro, f f
Haskell C P, Portland, 1 br, etc
Gore F E, Yarmouth, f f
Newell C D, Lisborn Falls, 1 br
Newell C S, Lisborn Falls, 1 br
Pumphray, E E. Dearborn, f f
Pickard John, Auburn, 1 br
Putnam, John F. Lewiston, f f
Richmond, C C, Monmouth, br, coch, etc
Sanders, L B, Bridgton, Langshans
Thomas, Melville, Brunswick, 1 br, w & b
    leg, etc
Whelden, L J, Bangor, lang
Whitcomb Rev. C F, Skowhegan, 1 br, p r,
    etc

MEXICO.

Demarest J D, New Laredo, f f
Espriosa Javier, Curvas, f f
Polosi, San Luis, f f

MISSISSIPPI.

Ford H C, Barndon, b leg
Hopper W W, DeKalp, g f
Hawkins H G, Enterprise, b c
Holsman C G, Wiona, p g

Kirk John M, Gunnison, g f
Perry A G, Olive Branch, g f
Shoemaker J S, Dakota, f f
Shoemaker C C, Freeport, p r, leg, etc
Sutton J E, Mose Point, bk lang, p r, etc
Scruggs W A , Mt Pleasant, f f
Whitley Joseph D, Cold Water, f f

MONTANA.

Schmid Gen, Phillipsburg, f f
Schmid Theodore, Phillipsburg, f f

NEBRASKA.

Armstrong Wm A, Greenwood, w & p r
Arnold W H, Verdon, b lang, w p r, etc
Brokaw Mrs M, Reynolds, f f
Brown Mrs R I, Elm Creek, f f
Batduf C H, Omaha, p r, p coch
Baker D W, North Platte, f f
Baker John, Swanton, f f
Baker E F, Swanton, f f
Baldwin Frank, De Witt, f f
Burbaker J D, Sidney, f f
Crane C P, Big Springs, f f
Eggert Ed H, Aurora, f f
English N B, York, f f
Fritts J C, Blue Springs, s wy, p r
Flamen J E, Dakin, lang
Goodrich W H, Lincoln, f f
Grimes W P, McCook, f f
Gillespie C C, Beatrice, f f
Gurspacker J C, Grand Island, f f
Harris Lee, Lincoln, g, etc
Lewelling C M, Western, l br, wy
Lemen A, Lincoln, lang
Nalces A E, Maywood, f f
Neal J A, Pleasonton, f f
Osterhout Geo W, David City, b leg
Pratt & Welmer, Fremont, i g
Pollock C G, West Point, f f
Roberts S L, Tekamah, b o
Ribble C W, DeWitt, f f
Ren L C, Bellwood, p c, p r, leg, etc
Stonebarger Theodore, Shelton, f f
Steinmetz Jacob, McCook, f f
Swartz E C, York, l br, b lang, etc
Sunsher Z H, Emerald, b p r, etc
Soule I, Wahoo, w & p r, etc
Sellers Mrs G B, Broken Bow, f f
Tillion Mrs C, North Platte, f f
Tannahill Mrs L, Bellwood, l br, s c b leg
Yule Fred, Lincoln, f f

NEW JERSEY.

Abbott E P, Stillwater, f f
Andrus W J, Hackensack, la fleche,
Anthony J, Delaware, b b r g
Boyer Michael K, Hammonton, f f
Bernnell Bert, Crawford, f f
Beckett A T, Salem, s l wy
Bennett Wm, Newark, ham, pigs
Beatty Lewis C, Washington, leg, min,
Boch Noah W, Trenton, lang
Beckett A J, Salem, s l wy
Bowlby L H, Washington, f f
Brown A C, Franklin, f f
Bradbury W H H, Hammonton, leg
Boger M K, Hammonton, lang
Brown A C, Franklin, lang, p r
Buzby M H, Masonville, f f
Cooper C S, Schraalenburgh, w & s wy,
  w p r
Church J E, Hackensack, pea c b p r

Cornish A W, Metuchan, s c b leg, etc
Clark J B, Vineland, f f
Camston Wm H, Phillipsburg,
Dodd S H, Orange, lang
Dorland L W, High Bridge, f f
DeForest A V N, Metuchan, f f
Drevenstedt J H, Jamesbury, i f
Dale James F, Trenton, p r, jap ban
Dougherty Charles R, Absecon, f f
Drevenstedt P H, Jamesbury, f f
Eakens John J, Patterson, f f
Eagle Rock Poultry Yards, E Orange,
  leg, w p r
Evans Geo C, Plainfield, f f
Edwards Charles L, Long Branch City,
  lang
Ferguson W E, E Orange, lang
Filler G W, Newark, pig
Fox B A, Hammonton, b leg
Frey W H Jr, Milltown, f f
Fiske J W, Passaic, leg
Fowler Dennis L, Jersey City, f f
Giddes Fannie A, Martinsville, f f
Gulde Chas M, Deal Beach, p r
Green Theodore P, Woodbury, f f
Haynes John C, Anandale, lang
Heller J, Newark, f f
Hawthorne Charles, Verona, lang, w p r,
  min
Hiles G, Mt Vernon, lang, b min
Haines C T, Crosswicks, wy br, etc
Hales Henry, Ridgewood, dor, i g
Holcombe Wm M, Readville, lang, wy, etc
Holmes J H, Crosswicks, w p r
Hummel W L, Shiloh, p c
Hofler F W, Morristown, p r
Hewitt W N, Bridgeton, l br
Hill T Wilton, Jamesburg, wy, p r, etc
Headly & Day, Union, br, dom, leg,
  etc
Hill Wilton, Jamesburg, f f
Hogan John, Newtons, ban
Hains W H, Philipsburg, f f
Holcombe Wm M, Readville, lang
Jacobs P H, Hammonton, f f
Johnson C W, Crawford, wy
Johnson Wm H, Hackensack, f f
Judd J W, Orange, f f
Kennedy W H, Camden, f f
Kayser Henry, Haddonfield, p c, l br
Keasbey & Co, Perth Amboy, f f
Lanterman J H, Blairstown, s c w leg
Lane Frank C, Long Branch, f f
Lidd A, Delaware, f f
Miller Mrs Henry, Plainfield, f f
McFerson John R, Belle Mead Farm, f f
Miller Percy, Pompton, f f
Morse W M, Elizabeth, f f
Milford L S, Vineland, min, coch
Mead W E, Hanover, f f
Nichols H F, Hoboken, f f
Oak Park Stock Farm, Hammonton, lang,
  p r, wy
Pressey G W, Hammonton, lang
Purdue Geo, E Orange, l br
Powell D C, Yardville, i g, l br
Phillip C B, Hurffville, dk br
Roberts Elizapeth S, Keansburg, f f
Richards Capt, Hammonton, f f
Read Roland, Colts Neck, rouen ducks
Rice Geo C, Blanstown, min, lang, leg
Roe Charles J, Newton, jap silky f

IF YOU WISH

TO - IMPROVE - YOUR - STOCK

why not get something first-class to do it with? Without a doubt

A. A. FILLEBROWN

HAS SOME OF THE FINEST

White Plymouth Rocks

IN THE COUNTRY.

A Postal Card addressed to him will bring you a Descriptive Circular, with prices, and your time and money will not be unwisely spent . .

A. A. FILLEBROWN,

AYER, MASS.

White Plymouth Rocks

A SPECIALTY.

ALSO BARRED PLYMOUTH ROCKS, LIGHT BRAHMAS AND PEKIN DUCKS.

Richmond J R, Yardville, l br p r
Rackham T Farrer, E Orange, f f
Roanoke Poultry Yards, Hurfville, f f
Rogers C E, New Market, f f
Rowland F, Woodbridge, f f
Reid C A, Englishtown, l & d br, p r, leg, coch
Schultz J H E, Mountain View, lang
Stafford Welsley R, Kirkwood, f f
Seaman Robert, Jericho, f f
Smith Willard, Passaic, lang
Smith E H, Salem, leg, p r, wy, p ducks
Shields James L, Washington, lang, min, wy, p r, red caps
Shamfanore, W W, Little Silver, g f
Spencer Stephen, Morris Plains, l br, p r, p ducks
Swann T W, Hammonton, br leg
Thompson C W, Salem, leg
Terhune Nicholas, River Edge, Hackensack, f f
Taylor Wm H, Rutherford, f f
Teaver Geo D, 1105 Bergen Ave, f f
Todd J H, Roseville, b c
Undall Geo, Jr, Morristown, leg, b c
Vail F E, Jersey City, f f
Vanderhooven R, Rahway, pig, lang, wy, p r
Van Mater John, Colts Neck, f f
Willow Run Poultry Farm, Clover Hill, lang, p r
William Miss, Hammonton, f f
Wheeler, E P, Salem, wy
Warne Jas S, Washington, i g
Waite Geo W, Jersey City, f f
Woolson Geo C, Passaic, f f
Wright Jos H, Trenton, f f
Young J W, Clover Hill, lang, p r

NEW YORK.

Alfred Allen, Newburgh, f f
Adams Newton, Utica, d br
Austin E K, Flatbush, b c, ban
Asiatic Poultry Yards, Box No 96, Hamburg, Erie Co, f f
Allen John, West New Brighton, Staten Island, p r, & w leg
Alstine D Van, Warners, b c
Alger F, Alden, w & b wy
Abbott Isaac, Freys Bush, b b red games
Alserley Charles H, Tonawanda, l br
Adams T F, Binghamton, g polish
Allen O B, East Chatham, w min
Anscombe George W, Saratoga Springs
Atkins R, Esopus, lang
Brady C A, Bloomfield, lang
Bacon Henry, Goshen, lang
Barnum W M, Angelica, lang
Bostick John, Commack, Suffolk Co, f f
Brown Homer J, Hartford, w leg
Brettingham J W, Stony Brook, f f
Burrell G C, Canister, br & w p r
Bentley N, Conewango Valley, red pile g
Boyce G W, Elkdale, p g
Boeker H E & Co, Seneca Falls, w p r, p ducks, etc
Brookman Albert, Seneca Falls, f f
Barstow C F, Peekskill, homing pig
Bolt Albert, German, min, br, etc
Briggs B M, Dale, w wy
Blinn E B, Jamestown, g wy, etc
Blake John H, Canajoharie, p r, & l br

Bennington Charles, Garrettsville, lang
Burleigh J F, Vernon, leg
Bennett W J, Waterville, p r, s c br leg
Baird D S & Son, Johnstown, bk ham
Barker C H, Albany, bk wy
Blunk A E, Johnstown, s c dom, leg
Barber C H, Albany, tur, l br, etc
Bly's Stock Farm, Palmyra, f f
Bedell F G, Clinton Corners, wy, s c br leg
Brace W F, Victor, ham, leg
Boeker W E & Co, Seneca Fall, p r, wy, leg
Brown Geo, Jamaica, f f
Bacon Henry, Goshen, f f
Barton J W, Buffalo, f f
Bryant E L, & B B, Johnson's Creek, pol
Branday F C, Whitney's Point, bk min
Bryant M T, Sherburne, s c w leg, w wy
Boyer Michael K, Hammonton, lang
Barnum W M, Angelica, f f
Brady C A, Bloomfield, f f
Brown Merritt W, Quaker Springs, lang
Bicknell J Y, Buffalo, bk min, & i g
Burdick H S, Rome, f f
Benedict H E, Elmira, f f
Brackenburg Geo H, Amburg, buff wy
Blythecote Farm, Brainard, wy
Bailey M T, & Co, Goshen, l br, lang
Barney Earl, Schenectady, br & w leg
Black River Poultry Yards, coch, javas, etc
Bonman & Frayn, Elmira, Cornish i g
Beattie S O, St Andrews, red caps
Burdick H S, Rome, i g
Bostock J, Commack, f f
Bricknell J Y, Buffalo, f f
Barnes R A & Son, Oswego,
Brittingham J W, Stony Brook, f f
Bull Alfred W, Bullville, f f
Binckney Daniel, So Onondago, hou
Bolster Cyrus J, Rensselaesville, s c b leg
Brockner & Evans, New York City, f f
Burrell G C, Canister, br & p r
Bemiss R R, Canastata, b p r
Bookman Albert, Seneca Falls, tur
Barnes Bros, Wellsville, w p r
Baucker J J, Rochester, p & f pig
Burrell G C, Canister, l br, p r
Blessing C L B, Shrigerlands, geese, ducks, leg
Brown A J & Son, Oswego, f f
Brown Geo, Jamaica, lang
Brown Charles F, Canastata, lang
Coedwell Albert, Poughkeepsie, lang
Cookignham Geo, Bengall, lang
Clark H E, N Y Nat'l Ex Bank, lang
Carey Miss M E, Fishkill, lang
Carncross W L, Plainville, w min
Corley H, Newburgh, f f
Coyle Frank P, Rondout, g f
Cornwell Charles, Schnectady, g f
Clark John B, 108 w 98th St, f f
Cornish Albert, Moira, ban
Cothran J F, Saratoga, f f
Crocker Irving, Seneca Falls, i g
Cunningham & Blair, Chenango Bridge, min, etc
Choate C H, Batavia, r c & s c br leg
Cunningham W H, Chenango Bridge, wy, red caps
Carter D A, Utica, ban, ducks

IMPROVED
Excelsior
Incubator

Simple, Perfect, Self-Regulating.

HUNDREDS IN SUCCESSFUL OPERATION!

Guaranteed to Hatch Larger Percentage of Fertile Eggs
at less cost than any other hatcher.

Send six cents for Illustrated Catalogue.
Circulars Free.

GEO. H. STAHL,

PATENTEE AND SOLE MANUFACTURER,

Quincy, Ill.

Caylor F W, Quogue, i g
Crone G, Memphis, lang
Colwell F A, Sherburne, br, lang, b c
Card Eugene, Morris, l br
Curtis Geo, Onondaga
Cosman D H, Middle Hope, f f
Cothian J T, Greenwich, wy
Croffut W N, Binghampton, r & s c br leg
Callahan Wm H, Smithville, Genesee Co, leg
Centre Alfred, b min, etc
Cox James, 426 6th St, Brooklyn, i g
Cushing B L, Maple St, f f
Colgate Robert, Quogue, f f
Case J C, Peconig, f f
Clendenning Tom J, N Y City, f f
Chataqua Co Poultry Yards, Silver Creek, f f
Coe A E, Fredonia, w wy
Craft W S, Port Chester, w & p r, etc
Coffin, Zimmer & Co, Glen Falls, wy, p r, etc
Clark Judson H, Elmira, f f
Case Stephen, Jr, Minisink, leg & wy
Dreyo Dr E W, Montgomery, lang
Dorr Jas B, Little Falls, f f
Dexter J M, Camden, f f
Durl Geo A, German, p g
Drake L B, Sheldrake, g wy
Devine J H, Utica, leg, etc
Davey F H, Minisink, l & w wy
Dunbar Maurice L, So Richland, w c b p
Dunmore R, Franklin, w min
Davison W M, Frankfort, w c, g & s wy
Dawley F E, Syracuse, f f
Bailey Dr M H, Alsron, wy
Dimmock O P, Urnellenville, lang
Drevenstedt J H, N Y City, f f
Drew S C, Cuba, f f
Doty E F, Toronto, g b
Davidson J R, So Bethlehem, red caps
DeGrail J Teller, Amsterdam, w p r, etc
DeLaney N E, Mt Morris, tum
Dickinson F M & W H, Whitney's Point, w p r, etc
Doane A W, Gainesville, f f
Dennis John W, Trout Creek, p r, lang, etc
Earle C P, Gouverneur, ban
Eggleston Fred W, Whitesboro, p g
Ellis Robert, Schenectady, w wy
Evans Geo C, f f, lang
Erdman Wm A, Batavia, p g
Eldred M J, Berlin, p g
Edgett A B, Hornellsville, f f
Elliott E J, Waterport, f f
Elwood F E, Freys Bush, w leg
Eddy Brace G, Alden, red caps, etc
Force Isaac, Honeoye Falls, c
Farrington J H, Saratoga Springs, f f
Farrer F, Rackham, N Y City, f f
Fuller W A, Fultonville, bra
Fallinger Jno F, Rochester, w wy
First Premium Poultry Yards, Niskayuna l br, etc
Forsyth J, Oswego, b leg
Fritz C Lovis, Buffalo, w p r, w wy
Ford G W & Co, Elmira, f f
Fales H M, La Salle, f f
Ferris James M, Sandy Hill, p r
Flint J W, Scio, g
Fulton C H L,

Flayler O B, Poughkeepsie, p r, r c w leg
Fulton W A, Fultonville, d br
Fraser & Feely, Whitehall
Forest Geo, Rhinebeck, pig
Gates L E, N Bloomfield, f f
Gilbert S L, Lima, hou, p r, etc
Gray A F, Homeo, p r, bk min
Gifford W E, New Hartford, p r, g
Gaylor F W, Quogue, f f
Ginon John M, Jr, Seneca Falls, lang
Gould S F, Avon, andalusian
Gillius George H, Auburn, p g
Goggin Thomas, Fredonia, l br
Gillet S L, Lima, hou, red caps
Graham W A, Par Coch, w & b leg
Grant H A, Tarrytown, f f
Goodman Samuel, Irvington, f f
Gillet Charles B, Lebanon Springs, wy
Green Mrs N K, Richfield, wy, p r, etc
Graves Joe, Black River, wy, w & p r, etc
Griffin Charles M, Shelter Island, lang
Gordon C, Charlestown Four Corners, lang, l br
Guernsey Rev, E J, Castleton, wy
Garf C A, Martinville, w leg
Gennet Wm H, Watertown, b c, br leg
Griffing Charles W & Son, Shelter Island,
Grant W M, Johnstown, b w fantail
Gibbs Wm J, Silver Creek, w p r, etc
Gaion LeRoy P, Seneca Falls, f f
Garfield the Hen Man, Port Jackson, f f
Green C S, Alfred, b p red & r p g
Goggin Thomas, Fredonia, l br & w p r
Goodspeed C M, Skaneateler, min
Goldman T Fred, Brooklyn, homing pig
Ham Eugene, Verbank, w & p r
Howell Geo E, Howell's Depot, s wy
Hasper Geo W, Keeseville, l br, etc
Hannum H A, Cazenovia, i g
Hutton P W, Putnam, f f
Hazzard J E, Elmira, f f
Harvey Frank, Cortland, f f
Harker Charles R, Editor
House Will C, Amsterdam, f f
Hammond Arthur J, Geneva, i p d
Hilke J C, Canajoharie, s wy, etc
Hallock W W & Son, Sponk, p d & g
Hawkins W H, Oneonta, w p r
Hazard James E, Elmira, s s ham
Hull Geo F, New Lebanon, f f
Horton Stephen D, Peekskill, f f
Hudson C S, Baltimore Station, f f
Hawley James E,
Hays J R, Walden, g wy
Hart W C, Walden, b & w p r
Howells Geo E, Howells Depot, l wy
Huges E M, Albany, f f
Hyzer A L, Andes
Heath C Warren, Amsterdam, f f
Hilke J C, Canajoharie, pea comb p r
Hammerschuridt C, So Buffalo, i g
Herbst Fred G, Rochester, f f
Homan C M, Silver Creek, f f, w p r
Haviland Benj, Ilion, r c w leg
Holmes & Tomlinson, Syracuse, tum, fan, pou, etc
Howard C M, 232 West 74th St, w wy
Hallenbeck Lloyd, Catskill Station, b c
Hood Kent, Green, p r,
Harrington Bev Jas L, Eagle Mills, i g
Ingraham F B, Bwingbampton, f f
Joy John, Potsdam, g f

Johnston Geo E, New Paltz, b ham, w leg
Johnson A C, Mechanicsville, f f
Jones Dr H W, Waterville, b leg
Johnson Theodore, Silver Creek, w p r
Kellogg E B, Honeoye Falls, f f
Kelley J A. & P F, Ithaca, f f
Kirby E P, East Chatham, f f
Klensen M, Rochester, g f
King Wm, New Concord, f f
Kirby W J, East Chatham, w dor
Knapp Bros, Fabius, s c w leg, w wy
Knox J F, Hamburg, w & b lang, etc
Kilmer A C, Cobleshill, p r, pol, ban
Knapp Duane F, Threlk, f f
Kershaw F D, Pompey Centre, f f
Kreshern P J, Amsterdam, scotland blue
Kassell Abe, 56 Loew Ave, f f
Knapp B R, Cortland, w leg
Knapp Willard, Fabius, f f
Kelley Mrs C M, Newark, b lang
Keller Philo J, Buffalo, par coch, fox ter
Kirby Richard, 62 Cortland St, f f
Kellogg E B, Honeoye Falls, bk leg
King Clarence W, Fayette, tur
Koehler C A, 17 Dekalb Ave Brooklyn, jar, etc
Lewis Frank D & Bro, Amsterdam, ban
Lohl Phil, Haverstraw, f f
Long J C, Jr, 62 Cortland St, f f
Ludlow Thomas W, Yonkers, wy, hou
Latin Lount, Staatsburgh, l br, javas, etc
Leggett Wm P, Salt Point, l br, w & p r
Limmer F B, Gloversville, ban
Lavell F W, Canton, leg
Leely Chas L. Afton, f f
Lane J R, Fort Edward, w & b p r
Lobdell S S, Sherburne, g & s s ham
La Fontain, C H, Batvia, l & d br, etc
Lewis C S, Prattsburg, f f
Luce Nat E, Binghampton, l br & b c
Little Joseph, Lodi, red caps
Landon H S, Angola, l br
Lavender A P, Tompkins Cove, f f
Long J C, Jr, 90 Broad St, N Y City, f f
Langworthy Isaac M, Alfred Centre, f f
Lory J, Poughkeepsie, l br, p r, leg
Lawton Slayer Jos. Albany, w p r, etc
Myers A P, Mohawk, wy & coch
Matteson H I, Sherburne, p r
Miller Newell E, Schuyler, Herkimes Co, red caps
Moore G S, Trenton Falls, lang
Mosher Geo D, Johnstown, hou
Mull Dr P W, Ghent, Gr Dork, hou,
Majer W H, Newburgh, f f
Maybee N J, 297 East 46th s, f f
Miller T F, Mattituck, w wy, w p r
Morse L H, Newark, l br, bk p ban
Murdock C E, Nineveh, f f
Martin Dr, Otego, p r, s l, w wy
Mills W A, Port Chester, f f
Miller J A, Canajoharie
Mosher Chas H, Johnstown, p r
Miller Dr J J, Amsterdam, f f
Morphey Thomas, Amsterdam, l br
Mann D L, Camden, w p r
Mabie Charles A, Holley, w p r
Matteson H I, Sherburn, w leg
Merril H O, Felts Mills, wy
Miller J A, Canajoharie, bk ham
Morrison James, Tarrytown, c g pheas
Miles E L, Sag Harbor, p r

Mount F A, Cherry Creek, red caps
Mount D A, Princes Bay, f f
McElhemy Frank L, Black Creek, p r
Moore Dr Ed, Londonville, hom pig
Medford Wm B, Schaghtichoke
Merchant Rev O A, Chester, ban
Myers L H, Bethlehem Centre, w p r, etc
Moody W H, Elmira, bk ham
Moore G S, Trenton, F St, l br
McHardy D P, Rome, f f
Moore Edward, Albany, g f, p r, etc
Nothrup C D, Ellicottville, f f
Nothrup Geo H, Raceville, w p r, etc
Newell D E, Foot West 19th St, N Y City,
Norton Allen E, Alabama
Nelson O F, Amsterdam, w p r, w javas, etc
Northrup I H, Cherry Creek, g
Newell D E, Rochester, f f
Nellis J H, & Co, Canajoharie, wy
Nicholoy & Son W H, Newark, g wy
Nellis J H & Co, Canajoharie, g & s l wy
Norton T H, Camden, g wy
O'brian John, Sherburne, wy
Ordell & Johnson, Queensburg, l br w p r
Ostenhout James, Woodbarne, leg, p r
Peer Geo E, Rochester, jacobin pig
Phelps & Harper, Keenville, wy, leg, etc
Phelps C C Vernon, s c b leg
Peck Abijah C, Clifton Park, p r, br, leg etc
Palmer G M, Rome, red caps
Preston Geo A, Binghampton, p r, etc
Pugh Emery S, Utica, wy, bk min, etc
Pluck A E, Johnstown, b h red & red p g
Pleggett Wm, Salt Point, l br, p r
Peterson C A, Albany, br leg
Pinckney Daniel, South Onondago, hou
Powers Eugene, Cortland, f f
Pierce S J, South Jefferson, min, leg, etc
Paige L B, Binghampton, f f
Pearce M S, Washington Mills, w wy
Paulding D C, North Tarrytown, p g
Peace M S, Washington Mills, w wy
Perkins W S, Fanport, p r, wy, coch, lang
Phillips D H, Albany, leg, pol, wy, p r, coch
Payne W C, Middletown, lang
Peacock Chas L, Fanport, s & l wy
Pear Park Poultry Yards, S M Stowell, Alden
Persons & Phinney, Yorkshire Centre, f f
Parsoris F H, Binghampton, f f
Percy John C, Chatham, dom
Powell C E, Cloversville, dk br
Phelps Geo G, Jr, Mt Morris, f f
Quick Elmer E, Brooklyn, Pig
Quinner F B, Gloversville, w p ban
Ourlhot H J, Tribes Hill, w p r, ban
Rice John L, Rensselaerville, s g dork
Requa E L, Highland Mills, s c br, leg
Rockenstyre C E, Albany, ban
Rennie James, Chesholm St, N Y City, blk br, red caps, etc
Rightmyer & Plant, Randall, p g
Robbins Dr W E, Hamburg, f f
Richmond W E, Hamburg, i g
Reimer J F, Milgrove, f f
Reynaud G P, 8 Bowling Green, N Y City, f f
Reaqua E L, Highland Mills, f f
Reese David, Frankfort, b c

Weed Geo W, Hyde Park, coch, p r, etc
Weisbecher F, Ilion, f f
Whitney C S, Darien, p r, etc
Wood Geo P, Union Springs, f f
Young J W, Carr's Creek, f f
Young M M, Arcade, red caps
Zeh Marcus, Scholarie, f f

NEW HAMPSHIRE.

Burns Willis L, Milford, f f
Chesley H O, Center Barnstead, w p r
De La Croix, Louis, Hampton Falls, f f
Dow Geo Q, No Epping, f f
Daniel Warren F, Franklin, l h
Flanders C S, Concord, f f
Fitch C C, Milford, f f
Gray Sarah A, Dexter, f f
Gilley F C, Hudson, f f
Gunn Herbert N, Keene, f f
Hill John W, Hooksett, f f
Hayward, C E L, Hancock, f f
Kimball W H, Gossville, leg, ham, wy, min, ban
Lewis Adams, Pittsfield, lang
Morgan C S, Littleton, i g, etc
Melvin F O, Bradfort, f f
Mason O C, Keene, f f
Pierce A F, Winchester, pig, g h
Page Geo S, Munsonville, w w y
Pratt Preston, Nashua,
Robinson, A T, E Kingston, f f
Spaulding E R, Jaffrey, g
Sause F C, E Deny, lang
Sanborn, A L, Lake Village, p r
Sheomet Poultry Yards, Winchester, f f
Suncook Valley Poultry Yards, Manchester, ban & pig
Fenney F S, Peterboro, g wy
Thomas Wm Arthur, Milford, ban
Wheeler Geo H, Manchester, ban & pig
Watson J F, Nashua, bra

NEW MEXICO.

Gillum J E, Catskill
Gall Perry, San Marcial, w wy
Lowe W S, Alberquque
Jerndensle in J, San Marcial

NORTH CAROLINA.

Bray W H, New Berne, b c, lang
Barron E K & M, Jorsicot, p d
Elliot Mrs Mattie Hertford
Harrill. W D & Co, Ellenboro, p r
Harney J Selby, Elizabeth City, lang
Monroe J A, Lumber Bridge, g
Stubbs J C, Rockingham, p r, p g
Welsh Dr S J, Monroe, br, wy, etc

OREGON.

Brown Carl F, Portland, f f
Borsch Wm, Portland, f f
Barret Mrs, Tre Salles, f f
Crain F W, Eugene City, f f
Camfield Chas, Oregon, f f
Dellard S L, Dellard, f f
George J S, Harrisburg, f f
Gay H C, Crawley, f f
Garrison J M, Forest Grove, f f
Henkle E A, Independence, f f
Kochen C, Amora, f f
Ladd E J, Portland, f f
Rose D M, Puggallup, f f
Suttle Geo, Portland, f f

Shum G O, Forest Grove, f f
Whittaker Robert, Salem, f f

OHIO.

Allen W A, Hapersfield, f f
Andrews Olive, Niles, f f
Arudt Ada L, Mrs, Sullivan, p r
Arnold Aug D, Dillsbury, f f
Allison John, Welcome, s wy, etc
Bassett E Meilan, w wy
Braden Robt A, Dayton, f f
Bridge A H, Columbus, f f
Bell J M, 201 Gooding Ave, Columbus, wy
Barney Wm C, 130 Croton St, Cleveland, f f
Boyle N, Mt Gilead, f f
Balthaser B, Amanda, s s ham
Barnes P Y, Shiloh, p r, br leg
Boyle Ed N, Mt Gilead, r c w leg, bk min
Burgbacker Wm, Chatfield, f f
Boynton Pliny A, Caledonia, f f
Buchanan Geo B, Liberty Centre, f f
Bursgan E A, New London,
Black C R, Cable, p r
Betz David S, Leetonia, s c b leg
Byard W C, Walnut Hills, f f
Byler D K, Urbana, 1 br, etc
Butts C F, No. Jackson, p r, etc
Barker B P, & Son, Colebrook, f f
Braden Robert A, Dayton, f f
Bauer Jacob, Kilbuck, f f
Brosins T J, Tiffin, f f
Blair F D, Georgetown, w lang
Bulley R H, Canton, i g
Boyd Wm J, Cleveland, red caps
Brassens F G, Teffen, f f
Bridge H A, Columbus, f f
Brown Otis, Jamestown, lang
Clifton James M, Sandusky, lang
Cary A L, Bishopsville, leg, ham
Cole Lucy, Harmar, red caps
Carroll T W, Mentor, Cornish i g
Chance T H, Fostonia, bk coch
Clemens F M, Jr, Mechanicsburg, bk wy
Cook W W, Perry, s c b leg
Chatfield W S, Woodstock, p rocks
Corlus Geo D, Atlanta, p coch, etc
Chapman F A, Wellington, f f
Chittenden W A, Whittlesey, f f
Clark R C, Washington, w wy
Chase Charles M, Portsmouth, f f
Crowell Wm, Clyde, f f
Craig Wm, New Burlington, f f
Cooper Arthur E, Ashtabula, f f
Cunningham & Hartes, 294 W Market St, f f
Cone A W, Painesville, f f
Clever Ed, Bloomingburd, Fayette Co, f f
Cox H D, Pleasant Hill, l br
Dewitt J F, i g
DeBang Johan G, Coal Grove, i g
Dun D D, Dudlin, l br
Dilker Charles, 25 Patterson St, Dayton, f f
Danbes Fred, Ravenna, f f
Doty Frank, Middletown, javas
Dalbey Bros, Washington, wy
Danes S B, Groveport, lang
Eaton Frank A, Bluffton, l br
Fisher Wm C, Butler Co, Collinaville, w wy
Fell E W & Co, 49 Wilbur St, Cleveland, f f

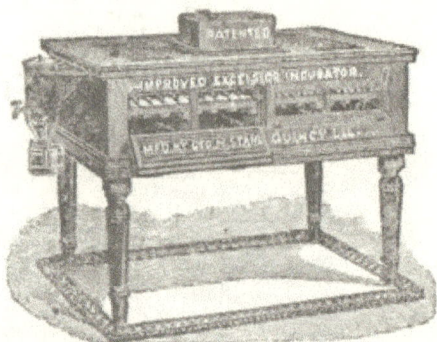

45

Foust T A, Dawson, f f
Fisher W B, Harrison, f f
Foote Bros, Medina, Ham
Farmer Joe, Flushing, Belmont County, f f
Falkner Thomas S, Tiffin, g f
Fletcher Jack, Franklin, b c
Fey F P, Cleveland, f f
Gilbert Mrs W C, Mentor, f f
Grove J W, Taulton, f f
Gilbert L M, Mentor, Lake Co, red caps
Gammerdinger Chas, Columbus, f f
Gave Charles, Columbus, f f
Graff H C, Kensington, n tur
Gulliford & Son, Akron, ban
Hodgman R N, Box 25, Parma, leg, ham, etc
Heyman M W, Massillon, b p r
Hodge J R, Mechanicsburg, wy
Heffernan L H, Forest, i g
Hathaway Wick B, Painesville, buff leg, red caps
Hinsdale W B, Wadsworth, br, coch, leg,
Hungerford L W, Painesville, s s ham coch
Hopper Charles, Aspley, p r
Hawk K S, Mechanicsburg, l br
High Harry, Amanda, f f
Harbaugh A H, Casstown, wy
Heirgardner A, Lorain, br, coch, etc
Haines D D, Geneva, w dor
Hagerman E H, Goshen, f f
Hawkinson W C, f f
Hananes J C, Cincinnati, p r & s c
Jones T T, Prospect, buff c, etc
Jones F M, Clay Centre, l br, etc
Jones E E, Addison, Gallia Co, l br
Jones Edward H, Ashtabula, f pig
Jones J H, Middletown, i g
Johnston Harry W, South Point, f f
Kohli D J, Bluffton, l br, coch, etc
Keller Ira C, Prospect, wy
Kelley P J, Tiffin, 217 Coe St, f f
King W S, Cincin, f f
Kenan & Pool, Upper Sandusky, l & d br
Keller P J, Tiffin, p coch, i g, etc p s
Lienhard Charles, 438 W Court St, Cincin, f f
Leffel Col J, Springfield, t f
Lowmaster L A, Belle Vernon, f f
Lee M F, Columbus, f f
Lawrence C B, Peru, f f
Lefler, C W, Marion, p coch
Lambers B H, Dayton, p coch
Lowry Oscar, Montpelier, f f
Lindes J W, La Carne
McCreight M C, McCullough, Adams Co, f f
Morris & Rodgers, Huntsville, ham
Marshall F J, Middletown, p r, etc
Mickey Don, 397 Fremont St, Fostoria, f f
McGreen T F, Springfield, buff c
Moore E A, Cleveland, f f
Meyers C E, Stoutsville, w & b leg, lang
Meyers Peter, Stoutsville, p d, p c, p r
Meyers Wm, Springfield, l br
Moulton C, Dayton, g f
McCabe Wm, Kelsey, Belmont Co, w p r, red caps & s wy
Miller C B Box 321, Dayton, wy, & p r
Martin J P, Bookwalter, f f
Mowry A J, Milan, f f
Miller A, North Georgetown, f f
Murray Wm, Mt Gilead, w p r

McLaughlin R J, Station B, Cleveland, f f
Morse Nathan, Akron, p r, b min
Mayhew C W, North Bristol, w wy
Morgan H W, Ashtabula
Myers Geo G, Walnut Hill, l br, p r, etc
Money H R, Prospect, wy, coch, etc
Miller Abram, North Georgetown, l g
Nye A L, Tiro, ducks, etc
Neff J M, Covington, rabbits, guinea pig
Newton J V, Toledo, w leg, w coch, etc
Naylor W T, Painesville, f f
Nixon L C, Ft Ancient, p r, etc
Osler P, Batesville, g wy
Orr W J, Urnopolis, l br, etc
Paul T D, Akron, f f
Pierce E F, Catawla Island, p r
Pricket O D, Shelby, s p & g p hamburgs
Parvis Miller, Cardington, f f
Proctor R A, Troy, w & b p r
Porter Willis, Hollanburg, f f
Price W F, Cleveland, f f
Pope S A, Bloomington, f f
Pickett Perley, Barnesville, p r
Parker E W, 1325 West First St, Dayton, p r
Robbins I M, Sidney, Shelby Co, p r
J L, Randolph, Bartlett, r o b leg,
Richley G H, Kennonsburg, f f
Richardson W J, Steibenville, f f
Roberts Dan, Youngstown, Cottonwoods, dom, etc
Saunders Percy, Richwood, f f
Shauley John R, New Paris, Preble Co, f f
Sheets Mary E, Conroy P O, f f
Singer Geo S, Cardington, f f
Sears A F, Wadsworth, f f
Shawl Earl, Bloomingburg, b coch, & l br
Simmons Wm F, Kilgore, f f
Stearns H D, Olmsted Falls, f f
Sammerric Frank, Springfield, f f
Stephens Sidney, Canal Fulton, Stark Co, s sham
Sputzen Howard, Akron, w p r etc
Sanueing Frank, Springfield, f f
Sanford M C, Townsend, f f
Schwartz Simon, Avon, Lorain Co, f f
Stone A D, Lilly Chapel, f f
Scheid Theodore, Bluffton, l br, etc
Skeers J F, Rochester, ducks, etc
Smith P, New Phila, game, etc
Smith D A, Akron, bk min
Streiter D, Hilliard, p r, etc
Shoemaker F A, Cardington, p r, etc
Sugar Bottom Poultry Yards, Mechanicsburg
Simpkins Fred A, Youngstown, wy
Smith Carl, 72 Huffman Ave, Dayton, f f
Turck Henry, Elmwood Place, bk javas
Tormiley S S, Manetta, w p r, etc
Taylor W F, 280 Fullertown St, Newburg Station, Cleveland, f f
Tinker J A, 19 Herald St, Cleveland, bk min
Tuyner Geo W, Genoa, f f
Tibbals Jno S, Kent, f f
Tonner Chas J, Cincinnati, f f
Unkefer Wm B, Robertsville, f f
Woolverton S C, Clyde, b lang
Watts E S, Greenwich, s wy, etc
Whittemore N G, Akron, s s ham
Wehry W H, Eatore, w pr
Wogamon F M, New Weston, f f

Wiant Dr T C, Marion, f f
Whitmore & Haines, geneva, p r
Werntz W O, Osnaburg, f f
Woolverton S C, Clyde, f f
Weiss E H, Aron, f f
Willer C B, Maild Creek, s s ham, p r, etc
White A C, Norwalk, b leg, w p r
Young J Edward, 33 So Sixth St, Newark, f f

PENNSYLVANIA.

Arnold Dr, Aug, Pillsbury, lang
Allen Webster, Tidionte, 1 br
Adams E H, Ellwood, s wy
Arnold A D, Dillsburg, f f
Anders A H, Kulpsville, leg
Allen A P, Meadville, leg
Altland Frank P, Menges Mills, f f
Arms M E, Milton, red caps
Alden R F, Montrose, wy
Alleback A M, New Bethlehem, leg
Armstrong James, Pitsburgh, f f
Anthony J M, Oakland, leg, min
Bailey F L, Ardmore, birds, jacob
Bender James A, Everett, f g
Benning James, Jr, Pitsburgh, f f
Broadhead W J, Elk Lake, f f
Beham Clark, Oakland, spanish
Bame H W, Harmony tur, etc
Barkam H A, Tunkhannock, f f
Bryant Jas M, Philadelphia, f f
Boericke & Tafel, Philadelphia, f f
Bals J Frank, Philipsberg, p g
Bean F G, Fairview Village, lang, etc
Blest John T, Lewisville, leg
Bowen John F, Wellsboro, br, p r,
Brown M R, Brownsdale, f f
Bradford C J, Lower Merion, f f
Bathhurst H A, Penna Furnace, f f
Booland Rev J B, Buttercup, lang
Bainett P G, Spartanburg, 1 br
Burbaker A G, Denvers, wy
Bowen John F, Wellsboro, leg
Bals Frank, Phillipsburg, wy, etc
Bean Wrrren G, Providence Square, wy
Barman M M, Steeleville, f f
Bosler Joseph Jr, Carlisle, p r
Burpee W Atlee, Philadelphia, f f
Brown & Wadley, Bolingbroke, 1 br, etc
Berkes Charles A, Kennett Square, f f
Berker John, Kennett Square, f f
Beiles A S, Leacock, tum, pig
Bean Franklin G, Fanview Village, lang
Cond M B, Kennett Square, p r
Cloud R K, Kennett Square, f f
Cobb A L, Ariel, f f
Campbell J L, West Elizabeth, f f
Cruser W C, Montrose, f f
Clegrove J I & C B, Corry, wy, 1 br
Chandler E J, Kennett Square, f f
Curran Geo A, Chanceford, br, leg
Corsow G & W, Plym, Meeting, f f
Cloud E P, Kennett Square, lang
Carey C H, Grey's Mills, p g
Campbell & Son, Meadville, br
Connelly O F, Carlisle, pig
Clifton Farm, Kennet Square, f f
Cloud T M, Kennett Square, f f
Cloud W J Kennett Square, f f
Cloud Bros, Kennett Square, f f
Cochian J D, Brattonville, w wy
Cochrane W R, Pleasant Mount, wy

Cary F R, Tompkinsville, f f
Dana N B, Radnor, f f
Davis Arthur A, Clarks Creen, f f
Dempwolf C H, & Co, York f f
DeWitt C H, Weatherly, f f
Denegoe Wm P, Philadelphia, f f
DeTuck P S, Kutztown, f f
Delwin & Wells, 305 Walnut St, Philadelphia, leg
Erich Henry, Allentown, lang
Enty G & P, Templeton, wy, & 1 br
Eklund John, No Warren, g wy
Eberle Fred W, Girardville, min
Everett W F, Westfield, leg, w wy
Early Sun Poultry Yards, Adamstown, f f
Eckert Anthony, Carlisle, p r
Fry Chas H, York, f f
Fredericks Bros, Eric, f f
Francisco C L, Sayree, f f
Fieles & Bros, Christiania, tum, etc
Frayn & Bowman, Elmira, f f
Foy W E, Lewisville, w leg
Frank Albert, Chatham, f f
Fleming O S, Bellwood, f f
Fonch A J, Warren, g wy
Fell Byron M, Mechanics Valley, br
File Chas H, Ronnsville, lang
Filbert Dr L S, Philadelphia, p r
Gannon T, New Cumberland, f f
Gibbons W & Co, West Chester, f f
Groves A P, Chestnut Hill, Philadelphia, w wy
Gallagher Andrew M, Norristown, wy, p r
Gram B F, Cordelia, g f
Garhart D M, Aitch, f f
Graystone Poultry Yards, Carlisle, f f
Green Valley Poultry Yards, Adamstown, f f
German F B, Millvile, leg
Gernerd C W B, Allenstown, br, coch, etc
Gamble Robert H, Bridgeton, f f
Hafer W F, New Columbia, f f
Hartwell Sherman, Washington, tur
Helpman J L, Homewood, w f b span
Harris C, Venango, w p r, wy, java
Hutchinson C G, Mechanicsburg, hou, p r
Hertzler J A, Carlisle, p r, etc
Hartton Joe B, New Castle, p r
Hoskins A B, Glen Riddle, jacobins
Horton H J, Belleville, f f
Heagy J, Trindlespring, p r, etc
Hope F, 464 N Ninth St, Philadelphia, pig
Hull H W, Tidiont, gol wy
Hollinger Jos D, Mastersonville, 1 br, p r
Hanzen H E, Hosensack, lang
Howe R C, New Castle, w fan pig
Humberger John R, Chestnut Hill, Philadelphia, f f
Hull H W, Tidional, g wy
Hickman Geo B, West Chester, f f
Heffley P, Somersett, g f
Hoch J C, New Maysville, f f
Hall L K, Brownsburg, f f
Huber W T, Bethlehem, f f
Hugger J F, Erie, f f
Hutton Joe E, New Castle, p r
Hensphill T Wills, Glen Mills, f f
Hagen Will H, Scranton, f f
Hanzen H E, Hosensack, lang
Kennels Memthon, Phoenxville, p r
Kester Joseph K, Kennett Square, w wy

Keller & Lebzelter, Johnstown, min. p r
Keyser A C, Lower Providence, f f
Kneger A C, Wrightsville, p g
Kerns Frank P, Chalfont, red caps. etc
Kulp W W, Pottstown, leg, w p r
Kurtz S J, Sanatoga, f f
Keller Frank H, Elizabethtown, br
King W W, Mechanicsburg, g, ham, etc
Kurtz A A, Emporium, leg
Kenderdine L R, Newton, p r
Keystone Poultry Yards, Blue Ball, wy, leg
Landreth D & Sons, Philadelphia, f f
Lewis Geo N, West Pittston, red g
Lawson Wm H, Honey Brook, i g
Lamont J M, Thompson, f f
Leidly M H, Blooming Glen, f f
Landwehr J C, Pittsburg, f f
Leader E J M, Philadelphia, f f
Mace W S, Towanda, f f
Mortimer Francis A, Pottsville, lang
McClellan R E, Christiana, p r
Mohr S K, Hilltown, wy, pr, leg
Miller J W, Craighead, 22 varietes of f f
Minner Henry R, Hereford, red caps, leg
  etc
Morris F, Norway, l br
McNary J R, Bugettstown, f f
Mayers H H, Florin, f f
Mullin A F, Mt Holly Springs, f f
Marsden Biddle R, Chestnut Hill, i g
Martin S J, Titusville, f f
Mehring John H, Littletown, p igeons
Moorhead Carl D, Brush Valley, f f
Maule Wm H, Philadelphia, f f
Malick Wesley, Platea, Japan g
Miller J S, Kessel Hill, leg
Mull J B Palm, f f
Mercer Jno I, Leaman Place, f f
Miller T F, Mattituck, p r, w wy
Mayo Jas, Pittston, ham
McCreary Ira G, New Castle, leg, wy
Moyer S C, Lansdale, br, p r
Mercer E P & Son, Kennett Square, f f
Marbin Howard S, Kemblesville, f f
Megargee M E, Kemblesville, f f
Noeckel H A, Landsdowne, hou, coch
Norton H C, Germantown, pig
Null S H, West Grove, f f
Nice James E, Jersey Shore, t f
Nichell Mattie E, Pickaway, f f
Newton A W, Montrose, leg
Nelson T M, Chambersburg, f f
Owens A T, Curwensville, p r
Orr W Harry, Reading, f f
Oak Hill Poultry Farm, Troy, p r
Oeth P M & Bro. Reading, ban
Purdue Geo. E Orange, l br
Plymouth Rock Yards, Carlisle, f f
Post R M, Black, f f
Price Frank, Troy, f f
Powell P, Clifton Heights, f f
Powell Thomas, 4716 Market St, Philadel-
  phia. f f
Payne Jerome, South Oil City, f f
Pressell E M, Derry Station, f f
Poultry Keeper Co, Parksburg, f f
Patton J H, Munson Station, min
Poole Charles H, Philadelphia, f f
Roberts J A, Malvern, buff c
Roberts Jesse, Erie, w min
Rice J W, Harmonsburg, w p r, bk lang
Rugh Samuel T Brush Valley, f f

Rittenhouse Jas. Smock, w lang, wy, min
Reese O D, Old Lionsville, f f
Rossiter Ide, Girard, p g
Ridall S F, Berwick, f f
Russel E L, Saegerstown, f f
Rush A S, West Middletown, f f
Rahner Rev F F, Waynesboro, f f
Spahr John, Waynesboro, f f
Spangler J, Rohrersville, f f
Sprout M S, Carlisle, f f
Sperry James M, Reading, f f
Sharpless Mrs Alfred, Landenberg, f f
Shangler J B, Mechanicsburg, f f
Showalter H A, Blue Ball, f f
Sullivan S C, Erie, l wy
Sweaver Thomas J, Jeannette, l br
Sharples N J. West Grove, lang, dom
Strong H m, Bradford, g f
Smith S W, Cochranville Co, f f
Sager K W, Irwin, f f
Shaffer W E, Nittany, f f
Stauffer F H. Union Deposit, f f
Searight Sue C, Carlisle, p r, lang
Storb H K, New Holland, p r, leg
Stokes John, 217Market St, Philadelphia.
  f f
Schofer F A, Reading, pigeons,
Stager Miles, Milton, f f
Swartley A S, Line Lexington, leg, wy,
  min etc
Strickler Harry, Greencastle, wh coch
Strong C R, Tidionte, gol wy
Schaller E S, Clark, bk lang
Schman Christian, Doylestown, f f
Taybor & Calvin, Experiment Mills, min,
  etc
Tyson Allen H, Lansdale, b min
Twinings Poultry Yards, Bucks Co, min.
  etc
Temple N G, Harrisburg, f f
Torkington C R, 4036 Locust St, Philadel-
  phia, pig
Tate E C, Everett, f f
Trenouth W, Sheffield, p g
Treichles A C, Elizabeth, l br
Temple N G. Pocopson, wh guin
Ulrich Geo R, Annville, f f
Unger J, Honsum, p r
Ulrich Geo B, Lebanon, f f
Vable H W, Philadelphia, pet stock
Vogelsong Samuel H, Hagerstown, f f
Vandivel John I, Philadelphia, f f
Velie H M, Condersport, wy
Watson J M, Jr, (Walton) Kennett Square,
  f f
Whitmer D H, Christiana, wy
Wonnan A J, Allentown, f f
Werner J M, Jr, Kennett, buff c
Whalon F C, Chalfont, leg, l br
Wilson Frank, Gatchollville, g f
Wigmore W H, 1078 8th St, Philadelphia.
  f f
Wimmer G W, Win, f f
Weidner W W, Bucks Co, f f
Weiner J G, Mohn's store, p r, etc
Wilson John, Chester, f f
Winters H H, Dunmore, f f
Walker D, Greensburg, lang
Wingate P, Wellsboro, l br
Yocum J O, Oaks, p r
Zimmerton J E, Pittston, f f
Ziverer H J, Lebanon, buff c

CLUBING LIST.

	Reg. Price.	With Directory.		Reg. Price.	With Directory.
The Fanciers' Review,	$ .35 per year,	$ .75	Journal,	$1.00	$1.40
The New England Fan-			The Game Fowl		
cier,	.50	.90	Monthly,	1.00	1.40
Poultry Herald,	.50	.90	The American Stock		
The Fancier' Herald,	.20	.65	Keeper,	2.00	2.40
The American Breeder,	1.00	1.40	California Orchard &		
Nest Egg,	.50	.90	Farm,	1.00	1.40
The Plowboy & Country			Poultry Monthly,	1.25	1.65
Farmer,	.50	.90	The American Breeder,	1.00	1.40
Southern Fancier,	.50	.90	The Southern Cultiva-		
Fanciers' Journal,	2.50	2.90	tor& Dixie Farmer,	1.00	1.40
The Western Poultry			Pierce's Poultry		
Journal,	.50	.90	Gazette,	1.00	1.40
Farmers' Review,	1.00	1.40	Poultry Bulletin,	1.00	1.40
The Iowa Farmer &			The Poulter,	.50	.90
Breeder,	.50	.90	American Poultry		
The American Farmer,	.50	.90	Journal,	1.00	1.40
The Poultry News,	.25	.60	Practical Poultryman,	.50	.90
The Western Poultry			Poultry in California,	.50	.90
Breeder,	.50	.90	American Farm News,	.25	.65
The Wichita Poultry			The Bee-Keepers' Ad-		
Home Monthly,	.50	.90	vance & Poultry-		
Farm Poultry,	.50	.90	men's Journal,	.50	.90
The Poultry Guide &			American Agricultu-		
Friend,	.25	.65	rist,	1.50	1.90
The American Poultry,	1.50	1.90	Ohio Poultry Journal,	1.00	1.40
The Poultry World,	1.25	1.65	Country Gentleman,	2.50	2.90
Pacific Farm & Stock			Poultry Keeper,	.50	.90

RHODE ISLAND.

Adams T H, Pawtucket, wy, br
Albro A M, Westerly, lang
Blake C E, East Providence, leg
Brown John, Greene, f f
Babcock H S, Providence, f f
Broomfield Ed, Pawtucket, f f
Brown Horatio A, Pawtucket f f
Barker J P, Newport, g f
Barker Isaac J, Newport, br, wy
Bentley J A, Shannock, g f
Brown & Hughes, Pawtucket, lang. i g
Briggs R I, Providence, lang
Burnson E W, Bristol, f f
Clarke F J, Peace Dale, i g, etc
Clarke E J, Newport, f pheas
Chase Mrs J. L., Newport, lang
Dawley H M, River Point, w leg
Davis R G, Providence, lang, p r, etc
Davis J Sanford, Pawtucket, lang
Francis J H, Westerly, f f
Flynn Michael, Jr, Bristol, f f
Gavitt Will C, Westerly, f f
Gardner R F, Narragansett Pier, s l, w wy
Hughes W M, Newport, lang, p r
Harts R B S, Providence, br
Lymansville Poultry Yards, Lymansville, f f
Lambert Daniel, Apponaug, b & w p r
Mallet Chas T, Pawtucket, f f
Mowry H W, Oak Lawn, w coch, p d
Manton D J, Lime Rock, p r
O K Poultry Yards, Pawtucket, i g
Palmer J F, Rockville, w p r, lang. etc
Robbins Joseph E, Central Falls, irish g
R I Poultry Yards, Pawtucket, lang, p r, etc
Sheldon W H, Pawtuxet, coch, & wy
Wilbur A S, E Providence, f f
Waterman Rufus, Jr, E Greenwich, f f
Watson Frank, Peace Dale, f f

STATEN ISLAND.

Staten Island Poultry Farm, Green Ridge, leg

SOUTH CAROLINA.

Addy D W, Leesville, l br, p c, etc
Ball J Alwyn, So Atlantic Wharf, Charleston
Cullum J A, Ridge Springs, s l wy
Cook Henry P, Graniteville, w leg, etc
Connor E C, Hodges, w wy, b leg, etc
Dunlap R T, Lancaster, g
Edrd J K, Rightwell, f f
Gadsden John B, Summerville, w p r, leg
Hazard A P, Georgetown, lang
Hollie Chas A, Charleston, min, leg, etc
Lea Stephen T, Cokesburylan, p d
Lachriotte L C, Waverly Mills, p d
Lee Thos B, Landrum, wy, p g
McIrenes Benj, Jr, Charleston, f f
Maxwell Scott, Vancluse, wy
Mosley Mrs W A, Prosperity, wy, p r
McComb S G, Charleston, bk min
Mirus W E, Sumter, min. leg, etc
Pine Land Poultry Yards, Summerville, lang
Poag E E, Rock Hill, f f
Smith Foss A, Charleston, bk lang, javas, etc
Story James M, Camden, bk min

Schrock W A, Greenville, f f
Seigler H G, Ridge Springs, br, etc

TENNESSEE.

Ambrose J H, Nashville, f f
Barlow S P, Adamsville, f f
Barker James M, Nashville, leg
Cleaves B, Mt Juliet, t f
Engles Josie, Murfreesville, f f
Echles J F, Chattanooga, p g, etc
Fignera C H, Murfreesboro, lang
Fryar J F, E Nashville, f f
Geer H B, Nashville, g f
Gray A R, Nashville, lang
Grigg J W, Mt Juliet, p r, buff coch
Henzel H, Hornville, f f
Hulsey O W, Fayetteville, br, lang, etc
Hoff Wm E, Chattanooga, p g
Hogsett W A, Jackson, p r, buff coch
Holloway L P, Glass, f f
Huddleston G Perk, Lebanon, p g
Hager R F, Nashville, f f
Jordan W F, Lascassas, p g, dom, etc
Moores W L, Cyruston, p r, buff coch, etc
Mette Jos, Memphis, l br
Parker I L, Tracy City, l br, s wy, etc
Prewett A L, Culleoka, buff coch
Parks W H, Fayetteville, p r, l br, etc
Stickly & Co, Nashville, lang
Twett Ed C, Franklin, l br, p coch
Way A S, Chattanooga, f f
Walker W S, Ogden, f f

TEXAS.

Baugh C F, Abilene, l br, & w p r
Brown Vories P, Austin, w p r
Cresswill S J, Mt Calm, lang
Dubbs Emanuel, Mabeetie, f f
Flock H, Dallas, f f
Fry R L, McCoy, f f
Terrell S B, Granbury, wy, etc
Hindman Robt M, Terrell, f f
Houston E T, Austin, f f
McMillan J T, Chandler, f f
McReynolds J G, Neebesville, l br, lang, etc
McNamara P, Austin, f f
Raymond Chas P, Austin, lang
Riggs C R, San Antonio, f f
Robinson Wm M, Dallas, w min
Schmidt C W, Rosenburg, f f
Sherman Mrs L E, Sakado, f f
Shaw W L, LaGrange, lang
Tefteller C G, Dodd City, f f

UTAH.

Clark N M, Salt Lake, f f
Cully S, Salt Lake, f f
Carpenter E D, Castle Gate, f f
Chambers F W, Ogden, f f
Cox J H, Salt Lake, f f
Earle H W, Salt Lake, f f
Edwards J V, Salt Lake, f f
Richfold Christenson, Salt Lake, f f

VERMONT.

Arms W L, Springfield, red caps, leg
Arms Bendette L, Springfield, lang
Ballard F S, Burlington, f f
Baxter Horace, Swanton, g f
Davis Geo, E Montpelier, l br
Daniels H B, St Johnsbury, p r, b javas
Doud L S, New Haven, f f

Donner C E, Brattleboro, b b red g
Davis Geo, East Montpelier, br
Frost J O, Vernon, 30 var. f f
Gould F W, Ruland, f f
Halladay & Paris, Bellows Falls. w lang
Hyde Fred H, Poultney, b b r g, etc
Horton M L, Windsor, f f
Jones J W, Burlington, tur
Lord I. B, Burlington, g s ham
Manley A E, Brandon, f f
Miner S O, Brattleboro, min, s s ham
Mattison C S, So Shaftsbury, f f
Payne C C, So Randolph, g wy, w p r, ban
Phelps O W, Bellows Falls, f f
Roberts R W, Bennington, f f
Russell C E, E Middlebury, 1 br
Swett W L, St Johnsbury, red caps, b leg
Smith C J, Shaftsbury, gol wy
Shaw E Y, Burlington, f f
Turner W W, E Middleburg, w dor
Wheeler Chas P, Burlington, p r
Willcox Hunt G, E Middlebury, 1 br

VIRGINIA.

Aydelotte A T, 23 Noes St, Norfolk, f f
Bogert Mrs H C, Cartersville, f f
Buchanan Wm, Saltville, p r. etc
Bowman J M, Nokesville, p ducks
Ball Miss Maria L F, Hopeside, leg, lang
Ball Miss J M, Hopeside, w leg, geese, tur
Bowman A M, Salem, f f
Bowley G W, Winchester, lang
Carson J B & E W, Winder, lang
Cooper J B & E W, Winder, lang
Jones C T, Manchester, red quills
James R T, Goresville, i g
Leonard J M, Waynesboro, p r, lang, etc
Lacharins & Picht, Richmond, f f
Marks J W, Berryville, 1 br, lang
Mestrezat Walter A, Morgantown, f f
Owens W G, Richmond, f f
Pendleton M H, Nokesville, p ducks
Reid Mrs Sarah E, Cheriton, f f
Showalter D B, Dale Enterprise, f f
Styrom O M & Co, Norfolk, f f
Saunders Clyde W, Richmond, f f
Taylor W E, Richmond, s e br leg
Wilson H C, Lyndonville, p r
Warner N B, Hamlinton, buff c, etc
Wine A F, Mt Sidney, p r, etc
Wheeler R H, Oakville, i g

WEST VIRGINIA.

Butler William, Shenandoah Junction
Miller Mrs David D, Martinsburg
McColloch Georgia, Shawbreck, g
Ott Jas K P, Rippon
Rumborger T T, Dobbins

WYOMING,

Bason D C, Laramie City, f f
Somers G W, Evanston, f f

WASHINGTON.

Adams W Centralia, f f
Andrews W R, Cheney, f f
Anderson J A, Walla Walla, f f
Burgess C Seattle, f f
Bunt W T, Seattle, f f
Burlingame H, Centralia, f f
Baker Mrs C, Chicago, f f
Bayer Chester, Walla Walla, f f
Benson A L, Chicago, f f

Benson Andrew, Chicago, f f
Brooke George, Sprague, f f
Cassel C F, Chicago, f f
Curry A P, Spokane Falls, f f
Comegry H C, Snohwash, f f
Copping Miss D, Centralia, f f
Calligan Mrs G M, Phinney, f f
Dickenson E A, Chicago, f f
Davis D W, Vancouver, wy
Elensworth Wm, Walla Walla, f f
French A J, Addy, lang
Gregg D A, Walla Walla, f f
Hansan C M, Chicago, f f
Hall A D, Alderton, f f
Hill E K, Seattle, f f
Jacobs A T, Marysville, f f
Leather F, Seattle, f f
Lucas E, Centralia, f f
Meach Mrs J V, Whatcuna, f f
Mussett F S, Chicago, f f
Peterson John A, Walla Walla, f f
Reynolds S S, Walla Walla, f f
Smith H W, Snohwash, f f
Snyder Alfred, Snohwash, f f
Sparks Beney, Chicago, f f
Spencer Mary F, Long Beach, f f
Stilmant, Walla Walla, f f
Satheland G C, Chicago, f f
Taylor A, Chicago, f f
Warwick John, Walla Walla, f f
Wightman W W, Buena Vista, f f
Van Spike Samuel Walla Walla, f f

WISCONSIN.

Arkinson G Ed, Markeesare, lang
Buxton C L, Sparta, s & w wy
Burrows F E, Delvan, g & s wy, g s b ban
Brabazon J R, Delvan, f f
Byers Fred W, Monroe, br, g
Bickey & Collentine, Blanchardville, duck
    & tur
Blackhun John, Darlington, lang
Babcock Butler, Beaver Dane, f f
Cowler G H, Elkhorn, 1 br & p r
Cowler T D, Darien, b lang
Collie W R, Delaware, lang
Cleveland Frank C, Richland Center, p r,
    lang
Dunbar S J B, Elkhorn, b min, b lang, p r,
    & ducks
Davis D W, New Richmond, g wy
Fay J J, Star Prairie, min
Fletcher Mrs A, Knapp, lang
Graves F H, Viroqua, i g
Gile D A, Darien, f f
Gleave Mrs S E, Evansville, g p ham
Guthnecht Otto F, Mosel, f f
Healy C P, Mineral Point, duck wings,
    blue reds, etc
Kneune H A, Sheboygan, g wy, 1 br, etc
Kirman Bros, Whitewater, f f
Kroeger W J, 422 18th ave Milwankee, p d
Long Wm, Wankesha, f f
Leonard Frank, Nora, poultry
Mann Mrs A H, Neveho, tur, ducks, etc
Mansfield Fred C, Johnsons's Creek, g wy
Moorhouse F S, Elkhorn, g & s wy, leg,
    etc
Mckeen, Owen, g wy
Mansfield Wm, Johnson's Creek, g wy
Mueller Gust T, Columbus, red caps, leg
    etc

THE
Sunnyside * Poultry * Yards,

JOSEPH BASSETT, PROPRIETOR,
YARMOUTHPORT, - MASS.

Barred and White Plymouth Rocks,
Brown Leghorns, Light Brahmas,
Langshans, Pekin Ducks and Geese.

YOUNG STOCK FOR BREEDING OR EXHIBITION FOR SALE AFTER OCTOBER 1.

PRICES ACCORDING TO THE QUALITY OF STOCK YOU WISH.

ADDRESS

JOSEPH BASSETT,
Yarmouthport, Mass.,

For all Information concerning Prices of Stock or Eggs.

Oak Grove Poultry Yards, Plattsville, p d
Prince W F, Viroqua, s c b leg, etc
Parson Frank, Darlington, f f
Paul Geo, Plattsville, p r, leg
Shuman F P, LaCrosse, l br
Riverside Poultry Yard, LaCrosse, l br, p ducks
Rich & Yorgey, Honcin, s s ham, hou
Roberts E G, Ft Atkinson, br leg
Star Poultry Yards, 922 State St, LaCrosse, p coch
Stillman W M, Delavan, g f
Thelander N A, River Falls, br & buff leg etc
Warner, Fero & Co, Whitewater, f f
Wither W W, La Crosse, g f

IMPORTANT NOTICE!

I shall be pleased to receive notices of any Errors. Omissions, or Suggestions whereby a Second Edition of this Directory may be made an improvement on this; also would be grateful for any new names sent.

FRED. R. CROCKER.

Publisher.

OFFICE OF

The · Provincetown · Beacon.

LEADING CAPE COD WEEKLY NEWSPAPER.

Provincetown, Mass., Nov. 1st, 1891.

TO THE READERS OF THIS BOOK:

CAPE COD EGGS are known the world over and bring higher prices than the egg product of any other section.

CAPE COD POULTRYMEN are just beginning to learn that in order to get the best results it is necessary to get the very best strains of the very best breeds of birds. You can reach the Poultrymen of this section only through the local paper.

THE BEACON circulates more largely than any other paper in the poultry raising regions of Cape Cod.

We will insert your ad. in the BEACON at a reasonable rate. The paper will interest you, as it is a family paper containing bright and original stories, music, Talmage's sermons weekly, and thousands of attractions. It is often illustrated. $1.50 per year, in advance.

Beacon Publishing Co.

CHARLES W. SWIFT.

www.ingramcontent.com/pod-product-compliance
Lightning Source LLC
Chambersburg PA
CBHW031759090426
42739CB00008B/1076